Games, Ideas and Activities
for Primary PE

This book is due for return on or before the last date shown below.

Games, Ideas and Activities
Activities
for
Primary PE

Second edition

William Allen

PEARSON

Harlow, England • London • New York • Boston • San Francisco • Toronto • Sydney
Auckland • Singapore • Hong Kong • Tokyo • Seoul • Taipei • New Delhi
Cape Town • São Paulo • Mexico City • Madrid • Amsterdam • Munich • Paris • Milan

PEARSON EDUCATION LIMITED
Edinburgh Gate
Harlow CM20 2JE
United Kingdom
Tel: +44 (0)1279 623623
Web: www.pearson.com/uk

First published in 2009 (print)
Second edition published 2014 (print and electronic)

ISBN: 978-1-292-00100-5   (print)
       978-1-292-00105-0   (PDF)
       978-1-292-00128-9   (ePub)

British Library Cataloguing-in-Publication Data
A catalogue record for the print edition is available from the British Library

Library of Congress Cataloging-in-Publication Data
Allen, William (Physical education teacher)
  Games, ideas, and activities for primary PE / William Allen. -- Second edition.
    pages cm. -- (Classroom gems)
  ISBN 978-1-292-00100-5 (pbk.)
  1. Physical education for children. 2. Games. 3. Group games. 4. Educational games. I.
Title
  GV443.A465 2014
  372.86--dc23
                              2013014611

10 9 8 7 6 5 4 3 2 1
17 16 15 14 13

Print edition typeset in 8.5/12pt News Gothic BT by 30
Print edition printed in Malaysia (CTP-VVP)

NOTE THAT ANY PAGE CROSS-REFERENCES REFER TO THE PRINT EDITION

Contents

About the author

Following the success of the first edition of this book and his time spent working with schools; William has now entered the teaching profession. This book draws on the tried and tested methods he uses in his teaching as well as the ideas he has developed from observing other teachers and his time studying for a Primary GTP at the University of Wolverhampton. He also draws on his knowledge as a very well-qualified sports coach, his experiences as part of the Cardiff University Coaching Bursary scheme and his time spent coaching in the United States.

Introduction

The aim of the book is to present both the basic skills of PE, and the means of developing them, in a straightforward and uncomplicated fashion, to allow non-specialist PE teachers to deliver productive, progressive and enjoyable PE lessons.

The growing concern for the health of British children and the ever increasing problem of childhood obesity increases the importance of PE, as it is the only guaranteed exercise that many children will receive, and despite PE being an essential part of the national curriculum it is often overlooked by schools and teachers. Part of the reason for this is that it is perceived that the skills acquired and method of delivering them are very different from how things work in the classroom. As a result, it is common that the teaching of PE reverts to setting up a game or activity and then officiating it. This book is designed to help move beyond that. This book covers Games, Outdoor and Adventurous and Athletics activities and provides guidelines for teaching basic skills and using practices to develop them.

The enormous success of the 2012 Olympics provides the springboard to positively change sport *and* PE in the UK, with the latter forming an essential part of the drive towards creating a lasting legacy. The government has actively encouraged primary schools to undertake at least two hours of PE per week. The aim of this book is to provide ideas and activities to enable you as the teacher to make PE an enjoyable experience. The second edition includes new activities and adaptations of existing activities, but most significantly includes ideas to incorporate alternative sports into PE, through volleyball and handball.

The principles of learning for PE skills are the same as the fundamentals for any topic such as multiplication or phonics. When introducing a new concept, you present the skill in the simplest manner possible to ensure the fundamentals of the skill are acquired. You then gradually increase the difficulty and pressure with the aim of being able to perform the skill in a complicated situation (such as a game or competition). The speed at which different children pick up the skill will vary and once the basics of a skill are acquired there is the potential for boredom, which means that it is essential to differentiate. The skills and activities presented here are designed to facilitate this and the progressions and variations provide you with the tools to differentiate.

The need for differentiation is further increased by the fact that many students will receive specialist coaching and training outside of school and you, as the teacher, can inform the class that there are opportunities to practise and improve the skills you teach them in PE. Those who do participate outside of school can also be used as a model to perform skills when they are introduced; then as others develop the skill they can also be used.

This book is a guideline for teaching PE; it is not an instructional book and thus is flexible and adaptable to suit the needs of your group.

Resources and progressions are more of a guideline and should be tailored towards your group to ensure that where possible everyone is involved and active at all times. Space and class size may prevent everyone from being physically active at all times, but where this is an issue, you can set a task for some of the group to observe others and give them certain things to look for, and when you stop the active group asks the others what they found, what someone did well and even how someone could improve. This is also an ideal way of including those who are injured or have no kit. Such people can also be used as officials and score keepers.

Safety is paramount in PE and you should take every precaution necessary to ensure the safety of your group. This is part of the reason it is important to have control over the class, and you, as the teacher, should be confident in the knowledge that, if you needed to, you would be able to stop the group immediately should any problem arise.

As a teacher you set the tone for lesson, so if it is apparent that you do not want to teach PE, the class will pick up on this and the lesson will drag. However, if you are positive, get involved and actually teach PE enthusiastically, the class will feed off this and their enthusiasm for PE will increase accordingly. Where possible the same set up has been used for different activities, which allows you, as the teacher, to know where you should be observing from, and means that the group is concentrating on learning or developing the skill rather than having to come to terms with the space they are using.

Acknowledgements

I would like to once again thank Elizabeth Allen for her help, advice and for being a springboard off which to bounce ideas. Thank you also to Richard Allen and Abbots Farm Junior School for their work towards the first edition, as without it this book would never have happened. I would also like to thank Cerys Allen, for her help with the photos.

A special thank you to everyone at Middlemarch Junior school, specifically for their help with the photos but also generally with all the support they have given me over the past 18 months, it is massively appreciated.

Part 1
Key Stage 1

Introduction

The most important aspect of PE at Key Stage 1 is to get the group physically active. Enjoyment is also a huge facet of Key Stage 1 PE, as at this age PE is for many children the first experience of organised physical activity, and if taught incorrectly can create a negative attitude towards PE and can deter children from pursuing physical activity outside of school.

Key Stage 1 is about basic and fundamental skills and movements. There are a variety of programmes and ideas that can be supported by the Key Stage 1 section of the book. Key Stage 1 is the foundation for the development of fundamental motor skills, which are general skills that can then be developed into sport-specific skills during Key Stages 2 and 3. A common programme for these skills is the ABC (agility, balance and co-ordination) programme.

I have tried to make this section as adaptable as possible due to the fact that different schools take different approaches to teaching Key Stage 1 PE. A common example is the time given for PE lessons, with many taking the traditional 50 minutes to an hour lesson, but with some adopting a modern trend of having daily PE for just 10 minutes. The activities have been designed to be able to stand as individual ideas that could be used for 10 minutes or as ideas that can be extended or combined to form a full PE lesson.

Chapter 1
Key Stage 1

Body parts

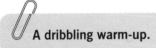

A dribbling warm-up.

Objectives

- To improve co-ordination through developing awareness of parts of the body.
- To get the group active.
- To increase awareness of body parts.

Resources

- 20 × 20m of space (and one ball per person if working with Key Stage 2)

What to do

1. Have everyone inside a 20 × 20m grid running around inside the grid trying to avoid each other. Anytime you say a part of the body, they have to put that part of the body on the floor.
2. Start with simple parts: hand; foot; bottom. Gradually work towards parts that require more control (shoulder or nose).

Variations

- This can be done with a ball to make this a warm-up for any Key Stage 2 invasion game either with the group dribbling individually or passing and moving with that part of the body being placed on the ball.
- Doing this can also be a progression for Key Stage 1 groups.

What have you bean?

This is an enjoyable and very active exercise.

Objectives

- To improve spatial awareness.
- To practise a range of movements.

Resources

- 20 × 20m of space

What to do

1. Set up a 20 × 20m grid and have the group jog around inside it.
2. There are different command words based on different types of bean.
   Each word has a corresponding action.
3. It is essential that you get into the spirit of this to keep a fast tempo.
4. Be as imaginative as possible:
   - RUNNER (run)
   - HAS (walk like you're old)
   - BAKED (lie down and pretend to sunbathe)
   - JELLY (wobble)
   - CHILLI (shiver)
   - FRENCH (kick your legs and point your toes while saying 'ooo la la'
     in a French accent)
   - HURT (rub knee as if you've fallen over)

Variations

- This can be used as a warm-up for Key Stage 2 activities.
- For the French bean you could instruct the group to speak in French to each
  other. This activity gives you the opportunity to create your own commands
  that can be tailored to your children and the work you are doing.

Foxes and hounds

An enjoyable, tag-like chasing game.

Objectives

- To develop spatial awareness and tactical thinking.
- To get the group physically active.

Resources

- 20 × 20m of space and bibs for all except two of the group

What to do

1. Set up a grid (ideally 20 × 20m) and then select two catchers (hounds). The rest of the group should be given a bib, which they place down the back of their shorts (to create a tail as they are foxes).
2. Everyone runs around inside the grid with the catchers trying to catch everyone by removing their tail. As soon as someone's tail has been removed they become a catcher.
3. The game ends once everyone has been caught.
4. Play the game more than once so that you can give several people a chance to be the catchers and the group has time to develop strategies.

Variations

- Rather than having it so once you are caught you join the catchers, you can work the drill so that once you are caught you replace the catcher by using the tail for yourself, meaning the number of catchers stays constant. If doing this I recommend using three catchers.
- This can be used in Key Stage 2 as an invasion game by including a ball to make it game-specific.

Monster tag

 An enjoyable tag game.

Objectives

- To improve spatial awareness.
- To improve tactical thinking.

Resources

- 20 × 20m of space and two bibs

What to do

1. Have everyone inside a 20 × 20m grid and select two people to be catchers and highlight them as catchers (ideally with bibs).
2. Everyone runs around staying inside the grid and the catchers try to tag them. Once tagged you stand still with your legs apart. To be set free someone has to crawl through your legs and then you carry on as before (this can be adapted to anything the group will appreciate).
3. Regularly swap the catchers around so everybody gets a go and to prevent fatigue.

Variation

- You can get creative and have relevant cartoon villains as catchers and everyone else as the cartoon hero, to add extra enjoyment to the activity.

The Borrowers

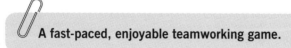

A fast-paced, enjoyable teamworking game.

Objectives

- To improve tactical thinking.
- To practise a range of movements.

Resources

- 20 × 20m of space, ten hoops (five of one colour and five of another) and as many bean bags as possible

What to do

1. Set up a 20 × 20m grid and scatter the hoops and bean bags around inside the grid. Then split the class into two teams and name them after the colours of the hoops.
2. Tell the group that they have to try to get as many bean bags as they can into their coloured hoops in the time given. You can only carry one bean bag at a time, you cannot take a bean bag from someone and you cannot stop someone from picking up or putting down a bean bag.
3. The main teaching point is to look and see where the bean bags are and then where the hoops are.
4. It is a good idea to play a series of shorter games, rather than one long game.

Variations

- This works just as well with more than two teams. If you have the coloured hoops to do so, you can use four teams so that there is greater competition for the bean bags.
- You can also use other objects such as balls in place of, or as well as, bean bags.
- If you are working with Key Stage 2, it is a good idea to limit the number of objects that can be in one hoop at any given time.

Remote control

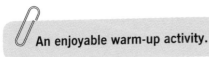

An enjoyable warm-up activity.

Objective

- To get the group physically active.

Resources

- 20 × 20m of space and if possible a remote control

What to do

1. Tell the group to find some space (an arm's length apart is a good starting point).
2. Then explain that the remote control you have is special and controls their actions and that every time you say a button there is an action they must perform to it.
   - Stop (stop and stand still)
   - Play (jog around)
   - Fast forward (run around)
   - Rewind (walk/run backwards)
   - Slow motion (walk in an exaggerated slow motion)
   - Record (freestyle)
   - Volume (up/down to control the noise being made)
   - Change channel (a hop)
   - Eject (a big jump)
   - Off (everyone falls down to the ground)
3. As you try the activity you and the group will probably come up with new ideas. The key is to find the commands and actions that suit your group.

Driving test

An enjoyable warm-up game.

Objective

- To practise a range of movements.

Resources

- 20 × 20m of space

What to do

1. Set up a 20 × 20m grid and have everyone find some space inside it.
2. Inform the group that they are all now cars and that this is their driving test. The important thing about a driving test is that you must not crash.
3. You then tell the group to drive their car at a walking pace inside the grid.
4. Then the pace quickens to a jog before finishing at running pace.
5. The norm is that children will circle the grid, and the driving analogy gives you an ideal way to stop this, as you don't drive your car just in circles.
6. The main teaching point is to look around so that you don't bump into others and so that you can see where the grid ends.

Variation

- This will work as a warm-up for any activity, but it is ideal to piece this together with the Traffic Lights activity in Key Stage 2 (see page 69).

I spy

An enjoyable interpretation and thinking game.

Objectives

- To get the group physically active.
- To increase awareness of surroundings.

What to do

1. The game is an adaptation of the children's game 'I spy'.
2. The equipment used is very flexible and it is a case of using anything that you have or can set up.
3. You say 'I spy, with my little eye, something that is . . .' and then you include a word or phrase, such as 'red' or 'round'. The group then look around and find something that matches this and run and stand by it.
4. Encourage the group not to just follow everyone else and reward and praise those who manage to think of things outside of the norm.
5. The objects can be anything from the wallpaper in the hall, the balls you may place around or anything which suitably matches the description you give.
6. Once the group is used to this they begin to really think abstractly, so that anything and everything becomes relevant.

Musical statues

A classic, enjoyable moving and stopping activity.

Objectives

- To practise a range of movements.
- To practise stopping on command.

Resources

- 20 × 20m of space and a tape player

What to do

1. Tell the group to find a space and tell them that whenever the music plays they must do what you say whether that be dance, run, hop, skip, etc.
2. When the music stops, they must stop.
3. If they manage to remain still when the music stops they score a point and everyone keeps track of their points.
4. If the group are moving around tell them that they must cover the whole of the space you are using and if they are moving on the spot have the group facing away from the tape player, as after a while the tendency is to watch the person controlling the tape player.

Head, shoulders, knees and toes

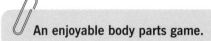

An enjoyable body parts game.

Objectives

- To practise a range of movements.
- To reinforce knowledge of body parts.

What to do

1. This works on the basis of the 'head, shoulders, knees and toes' song.
2. Have the class in a straight line with space between each person to allow for movement.
3. You go through the song and touch the part of the body you say. After a couple of goes, so that everyone gets the hang of the song, you gradually take the words out but still touch the body so that eventually all you are saying is 'and'. This is the fun part of the exercise.
4. You can vary the pace and tone of the exercise by telling the group to do it as quickly or as slowly as possible, or by doing it in funny voices, such as, as if you are Elvis (for which you put on an Elvis voice and wiggle your hips).

Variations

- A great variation for Key Stage 2 is to do it in a different language, such as French, or if you have a foreign-language-speaking child in your group you could ask them to lead the class.
- You could also set it as homework and ask the class to find the translation for a language of their choice. The French becomes (with toes changed to feet):

   'Tête, épaules, genoux et pieds, genoux et pieds. Tête, épaules, genoux et pieds, genoux et pieds. La bouche, le nez, les yeux, les oreilles. Tête, épaules, genoux et pieds, genoux et pieds.'

Whose ball is it anyway?

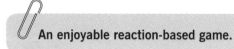 **An enjoyable reaction-based game.**

Objectives

- To practise a range of movements.
- To test reaction times.

Resources

- One ball per pair

What to do

1. Create a long line (using cones or tape) and split the class into pairs and have the pairs line up 1m either side of the line. Place a ball on the line between the pairs.
2. Tell the group that if you say a part of the body then they must touch that part of their body, and if you say an action they must perform it.
3. Anytime you say 'ball' they must grab their ball as quickly as possible with the aim of beating their partner.
4. Swap partners around so that they play against different people.

Variation

- A great addition is to say things such as balance or boots as the start of the sound starts the reaction and once someone moves others will react to their reaction.

Monsters Inc.

Objectives

- To practise a range of movements.
- To prepare the class for the lesson ahead.

Resources

- 20 × 20m of space

What to do

1. Explain the story of *Monsters Inc.* to the group (ideally some of the children will know it and can help you), that a long time ago energy companies used children's screams for energy and that monsters used to be sent to capture these screams. However, monsters are allergic to children so if touched by children the monsters fall ill.

2. There are various actions they perform based on what you say.
   - Scary feet (move from foot to foot as quickly as possible)
   - Kids awake (lie on the ground as quickly and as silently as possible)
   - Walk (walk around taking long strides as monsters do)
   - Run (run around in a similar fashion to the walk)
   - Kids coming (run to the edge of the space)

3. This works best when you are enthusiastic and although *Monsters Inc.* may become outdated with time, this gives you an idea of how it could be used for popular stories or movies that are more relevant.

Pirates of the sea

An enjoyable warm-up game.

Objectives

- To practise a range of movements.
- To prepare the class for further activities.

Resources

- 20 × 20m of space

What to do

1. Have the group find a space and tell them they are now on a pirate ship and they are all now pirates.
2. Explain to the group that you have a series of pirate commands that they must listen to. Introduce the different commands and actions one by one.
   - Pirates at work (group run around)
   - Scrub the deck (kneel down and pretend to scrub the floor)
   - Man overboard (jump as if falling overboard)
   - Walk the plank (walk slowly as if on a plank)
   - Climb the rigging (group pretend to climb)
   - Captain's coming (children salute and shout 'aye, aye cap'n')
   - Compass point (everyone runs to the middle of the room)
   - Land ahoy (children stop and look to the distance)
   - Man the lifeboats (sit down)
   - Numbers in lifeboats (the number you shout is the size of the groups the class has to get into)
3. There will be lots of possible variations of commands for this. Again ask the group and add ideas you think are suitable.

Teacher says

An enjoyable adaptation of the classic children's game 'Simon says'.

Objectives

- To practise a range of movements.
- To test listening skills.

What to do

1. Have the class spread out, but ensure that you can see everyone at all times.
2. The game works on the same basis as Simon says but you substitute Simon with your name.
3. Tell the class that whenever Mr, Mrs or Miss says for you to do something you must do it, but if you do not use your name then they should not do it.
4. Use commands such as stand still, run around, jog on the spot, stand on one leg and turn around. Use any commands that are suitable and see how difficult it is to catch people out.

Pass the buck

An enjoyable warm-up game.

Objective

* To get the group physically active.

Resources

* One ball

What to do

1. Have the group form a big circle (a good way to get the circle is to have the class hold hands).
2. You stand in the middle with your eyes closed (ensure that you have another adult with you to watch the group). You count to 20 (in your head) at varying speeds.
3. While you are counting, the group have to pass (throwing is not allowed) the ball around the circle. When you say 'now', whoever has the ball is out, and has to sit down on the floor with their legs stretched out together, straight ahead of them.
4. The 20 seconds will then restart and the group pass the ball around the circle. As the class approach the person who is out, they must take the ball in two hands and jump over the legs of the person that is out and pass the ball to the next person.
5. This may involve jumping over several people, so you have to ensure that there is a gap between each person and that the child jumps over one at a time and does so safely.
6. When you get to the final two, have them stand back to back, and every time you say a fruit they take a step forward, but if you say an animal they must stand still. The first person to move when they shouldn't loses.

Variations

- You can use more than one ball.
- Alternatively, you could set up smaller groups with children doing the counting.

Combat crawlers

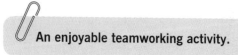

An enjoyable teamworking activity.

Objectives

- To get the group physically active.
- To get the group communicating with each other.

What to do

1. Split the group into teams of equal numbers, with at least six people in each team.
2. Have each team line up in single file. Each person should have their legs at least shoulder width apart and should be approximately 30cm behind the next person.
3. When you say 'go' the person at the back of the line crawls through everybody's legs until they reach the front. Once at the front they stand up and shout 'attention'.
4. The back person then crawls through again and the process is repeated. The winner is the first to team to get back into starting order.

Variation

- After this has been done twice, change it so that it is a competition to see who can get from one side of the hall to the other first just by doing this (this works well if you have uneven numbers in your teams).

Figure phonics

 A fun activity that also works on letter shape and sounds.

Objectives

- To get the group physically active.
- To reinforce the sounds and shapes of letters.

What to do

1. Have everyone find a space and then walk around the space you are using.
2. Every time you say a letter the group must stop and try to create that letter with their body (you can use upper and lower-case letters to progress the activity further). The group can work individually, with a partner or with you as a group. Every time you say a letter the group must repeat it.

Word game

A teamworking game that works on shape, movement and spelling.

Objectives

- To practise spelling.
- To be aware of shape while using teamwork.

Resources

- Card (showing the picture or action word)

What to do

1. There are several ways of working this and you can adapt it to suit the ability of the group and your aims.
2. Split the group into teams of between three and six. Set up a series of stations with a picture or action word placed at each station. The teams move around all of the stations. As they arrive at a station they look at the picture and then have to figure out the word and create it with their bodies. For very able groups, you can have the action word as a secret, so one group spells the word and another group has to guess the word.

Variations

- An alternative is to have the groups in separate spaces and give them a word to spell.
- Alternatively you could spell words in lower case and have the group spell them in capitals and vice versa, or even give the group digits to spell.
- This can be used in Key Stage 2 by using more advanced words or as a warm-up for gym sessions.

What I did this morning

An enjoyable activity that covers a variety of actions.

Objectives

- To get everyone active.
- To practise a range of movements.

What to do

1. Have everyone find space and instruct the group to copy all of your actions.
2. The story is that you are late for school so (while staying on the spot) you must go through all the actions needed to get ready and get to school as quickly as possible. This works best with you narrating the story and actually doing the actions. Be both energetic and dramatic.
3. Start by lying on the floor, then 'beep, beep, beep', the alarm goes. 'Oh no I'm going to be late for school!' So you quickly get up (jump to your feet), run downstairs (jog on the spot), brush your teeth, wash your face and put some clothes on (act all of these out). 'Oh I've left my bag upstairs' (so run back upstairs), pick up the bag and then run back downstairs. 'I'm hungry', so you pretend to eat some food.
4. Then you leave the house, so you open the door and begin to run to school (run on the spot). 'It's the road!' so you stop, look both ways and then walk across the road. You then begin to run again but come across a hedge that you have to jump over.
5. Then you arrive at school . . . only to find it's Saturday!!!

Variation

- This can be done for going to bed or any everyday activity.

Who did it?

A fun game that uses a range of movements.

Objectives

- To get the group physically active.
- To complete a range of movements.

What to do

1. Have everybody make a large circle.
2. Select one or two students to be the investigators. Have them stand in the middle of the circle.
3. Select a villain. The villain performs different exercises which the rest of the class follow. The investigators have to discover who the villain is. A good starting point is to give the investigators five guesses.
4. Tell the rest of the group that it is really important that they watch the villain so that they can react and respond quickly.

Number square

 A fun, active mathematical game for upper KS1.

Objectives

- To get the group physically active.
- To further number recognition.

Resources

- Numbers (or sums) on pieces of paper

What to do

1. Split the class into four groups and have each group stand in a corner of the hall (or outlined large space). Place a number (either numerical or written), in each corner to depict what number each corner represents.
2. Explain that any time you say 'number square', they have to come and sit in the middle as quickly (and carefully) as possible in organised rows and columns and that any time you say 'square', they go back to their starting corners.
3. If you say the numbers of two of the groups then those groups must swap positions, but it is important to warn the class that everyone will be running around so they must look where they are going.

Variation

- Use sums or number-based questions rather than just writing the questions. You could also have a pile or booklet of numbers or questions to vary the numbers you are using.

Part 2
Games

Introduction

Games

Most PE timetables give more time to games than the other sections of the national curriculum and this is due to the depth and breadth of the area. The aspects of games the national curriculum states should be covered are striking and fielding, net/wall and invasion.

The national curriculum states:

Pupils should be taught to:

- Play and make up small-sided and modified competitive net, striking/fielding and invasion games.
- Use skills and tactics and apply basic principles suitable for attacking and defending.
- Work with others to organise and keep the games going.

It is important not solely to officiate games, but to teach as well. In any typical class you will have many children who pursue a games activity outside of school and receive coaching. The problem this causes is that in any given class you can have a wide range of abilities (more so than normal). All of the drills used in this section can be adapted to suit a range of abilities and to support differentiated learning.

The way the book is designed is that in the games section we have the basic skills, an unopposed practice, opposed practices and then game-related practices and games themselves. These combine into a basic lesson plan whereby you have (for a 1-hour lesson), 10 minutes for the warm-up, 20 minutes working on basic skills and unopposed practices, 10 minutes of opposed practices and 15 minutes game-related, finishing with 5 minutes for a cool-down. Working in this structure allows for a lot of flexibility and means that you can advance the more able in the group on to the next activity (or a more complex version of the current one) and those that are struggling can be kept on the current activity. It also allows for the constant consideration of grouping, safety and organisation; the essential three considerations for every PE lesson.

Within the three areas of games there are sports and area-specific considerations to be made and these are highlighted in the introduction of each section. If children excel, are enthusiastic or ask about playing sport there are a multitude of local sports clubs and teams so that they can pursue sports outside of school as well.

Invasion

As the area of games with the highest proportion of children playing or receiving training outside of PE, this is the area wherein the ability range will be most widespread. It is therefore essential that you plan for differentiation within the class. A great teaching technique is to use the more able in the group as an asset to you, as the teacher. You can use the more able in the group as models for skills or tactics in the early stages so that their confidence is boosted and they become actively interested in the lesson. When you then use other people in the group as examples they feel they are beginning to reach the level of their more advanced peers.

A common problem is that the more advanced group members will want to do everything themselves and, while they show great skill in doing so, they are not showing tactical ability. So the challenge for the more advanced can be how to become a better team player and how to help teammates who may not be as able as themselves. When you achieve this, you actually work everyone in the group and everyone improves.

As part of the research for the lesson you should look up professional players and find professionals who excel at the sport and the skills you are teaching, as this helps those with active interest in the sport to be able to relate more closely to what you are trying to teach.

Chapter 2
Football

Push pass

 The fundamentals of the basic pass for football.

Objective

- To introduce passing with the inside of the foot.

Resources

- Enough balls for one ball and 5 × 5m of space for each pair

What to do

1. Place the non-kicking foot next to ball, so that the toe is in line with the middle of the ball and 7–10cm to the side. This foot should point in the direction you want the ball to go.
2. Bring the kicking foot backwards and swing the leg through, ensuring the non-kicking foot stays straight. It is the inside of the foot that should connect with the ball (as the large surface area provides greater control) (see Figure 2.1).
3. It is important that the ankle of the kicking foot remains firm and the contact is made with the middle of the ball.
4. The power or weight of the pass should depend on how far the ball has to travel, and is discovered with practice over time.
5. It is imperative to stress not to use the toes.
6. A simple practice is to have people stand in pairs and pass back and forth. A good starting distance is 5m, but this is dependent on the ability of the pair. To differentiate learning you can change the distances or make people use their non-preferred foot.

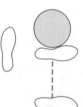

Figure 2.1 Football skills – the push pass.

Ball control

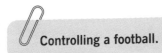

Controlling a football.

Objective

- To introduce the fundamental skill of controlling a football.

Resources

- Enough balls for one ball and 5 × 5m of space for each pair

What to do

1. There are several parts of the foot that can be used to control a ball, but the simplest and quickest method is using the inside of the foot.
2. You need to ensure that you are in line with the path of the ball.
3. Place your left foot to the side of where the ball is travelling. Your feet should be shoulder width apart with the right foot positioned just behind the left to create a 90° angle.
4. As the ball hits your foot your ankle should be locked but also provide a slight cushion. Ideally, your control will stop the ball in line with your left foot (as this then allows for a push pass (see left) without having to adjust the body).

Dribbling

The fundamentals of dribbling in football.

Objectives

- To introduce dribbling.
- To introduce various parts of the foot that can be used.

Resources

- 20 × 20m of space and one ball per person

What to do

1. There are various parts of the foot that can be used to dribble, the most common being the laces and the inside of the foot. Encourage the group to use a mixture of the different parts of the feet other than the toes.
2. The most important thing is that when dribbling the ball remains within reach (approximately a metre in front of the feet), so that you can stop the ball at any point.
3. In the early stages (cognitive phase) the aim is to be comfortable with the ball at your feet and to be aware of other players and pitch markings.
4. Encourage players to look up as much as possible to see what is around them. (A useful analogy is to ask them what would happen if they walked down the street with their head just looking at their feet, and to explain that the same idea applies to football.)
5. Have the group dribble around in a 20 × 20m grid. Ask them to use each part of the foot on its own, then allow them to use different combinations and eventually allow them to use them all as they choose.
6. Then have only half the group with a ball. Those with a ball dribble around and those who don't act as static defenders. After a while they switch roles.
7. Gradually increase the involvement of the defenders from walking, to jogging, to running and finishing with 100 per cent effort to get the ball.

Variation

- Ask them to use just one foot, then both, to give a practical example of the fact that it is easier to use both feet.

Shooting

The fundamentals of shooting with the laces.

Objective

- To introduce the basic shooting technique.

Resources

- Enough balls for one ball and 5 × 5m of space for each pair

What to do

1. Place your non-kicking foot next to the ball (approximately 7–10cm away), so that the tip of the foot is parallel with the middle of the ball. This foot should point in the direction you want to shoot the ball.
2. Bring the kicking foot backwards and swing the leg through, ensuring the non-kicking foot stays facing forwards. It is the laces of the boot that connect with the ball (as the bone at the top of the foot allows for greater power) and this is achieved through ensuring the toes are pointed downwards in a ballet-like manner.
3. It is important the ankle of the kicking foot remains firm and the contact is made with the middle of the ball.
4. The power or weight of the shot will depend on how far the ball has to travel, but this will be found out by the individual with practice over time.
5. It is imperative to stress that it is not the toes that make contact with the ball.
6. A good learning tool to use is the idea of toe, knee, chin (TONY CHIN). This is the idea that at the point of a strike your toes should be pointing downwards so that your toes, knee and head are in line.
7. Also stress the importance of keeping the ball low (head over the ball and not leaning back) and towards the corners.
8. A good practice is to divide the group into pairs, standing 5m apart, taking turns to be the shooter and goalkeeper.

Variations

- Adjust the distance depending on the ability of the player.
- Ask them to use their non-preferred foot.

Heading

The fundamentals of heading a football.

Objective

● To introduce the basic heading technique.

Resources

● Enough balls for one ball and 5 × 5m of space for each pair

What to do

1. The most important teaching point for heading is the fact that you must use the forehead. A good teaching tool is to ask what the forehead is used for, and then explain it is *for* . . . heading.
2. The next teaching points are to keep your eyes open (so you can see the ball) and your mouth closed (to prevent biting the tongue and lower the chance of a jaw injury).
3. As the ball approaches it is important that you move your head towards the ball rather than letting the ball hit your head. This requires you to use your neck and arms to propel yourself forwards when heading. A good teaching tool is to imagine climbing through a window.
4. The best way to practise this is to have pairs standing 5m apart and have them either throwing the ball for themselves or have their partner throw the ball, so that they can head the ball back to their partner.
5. It is ideal to stand at an angle. A good starting point would be to have one foot pointing straight and the other at a 90° angle; the front foot will point to where you want the ball to go, just as with passing and shooting.
6. An attacking header aims to get the ball low, whereas a defensive will be high and far.

Variation

- Once this has been mastered, have the group move around inside a 20 × 20m grid, jogging around while doing the throw and header.

Inside hook turn

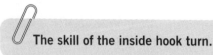

The skill of the inside hook turn.

Objective

- To introduce the inside hook turn as a means of changing direction.

Resources

- 20 × 20m of space and one ball per person

What to do

1. As you are dribbling with the ball have the ball just in front of your feet as instructed on page 34.
2. Bring the left foot forward so that it is about 15cm away from the right-hand side of the ball.
3. Bring the right foot around so that the inside of the foot is perpendicular to the left foot and then push the ball away with the inside of the right foot, swing the body around and then accelerate away.
4. Have the group inside a 20 × 20m grid practising this on their own.

Variation

- A good variation is the outside hook, which works on the basis of dribbling and having the ball in front of your feet. Bring the left foot in line with the left-hand side of the ball, but shoulder width away from it. Then bring the right foot around the left-hand side of the ball and place it on the ground so that creates the same angle as with the inside hook. This time the outside of the right foot should push the ball forwards and then twist the body around and accelerate away.

Scissors

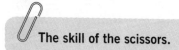

The skill of the scissors.

Objective

- To introduce the scissors as a means of beating a defender.

Resources

- One ball per person and 5 × 5m of space per pair

What to do

1. This is an advanced skill that can be learnt easily but, as with any skill, it is important to know when to use it, which in this case is when you are trying to beat a defender.
2. Dribble towards the defender until you are about 1.3–1.8m away from them.
3. Pick a side you want to move to. The skill involves a feint in the opposite direction and then moving in the direction you want to.
4. If you are moving to the right, feint left. For the feint, bring your left foot around the ball from inside to out, keeping your foot close to the ground as if to cut the grass (as with scissors), then plant the foot in the position it started in.
5. Push the ball away with the outside of the right foot and move past the defender. The quicker the transaction from feint to real move, the more effective the skill will be, as the defender has less time to readjust body position.
6. To move in the opposite direction, feint with the right foot and push with the left.
7. It is hugely important that, when the ball is moved away, you accelerate away in order to move past the defender.

⭐ Variation

- Have the group in pairs inside 5 × 5m channels, both start on a side facing each other, they then dribble to the middle of the grid and move away from each other.

Head catch

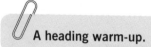

A heading warm-up.

Objective

* To prepare for a heading session.

Resources

* One ball

What to do

1. Get everyone in a big circle and stand in the middle of it.
2. To begin with you will throw the ball to individuals and say either 'head' or 'catch' and, whichever command you give, they have to do it.
3. That should be pretty straightforward, so after everyone has had a correct attempt change the instructions so that every time you say 'head', they catch, and every time you say 'catch', they head.
4. There are several ways to run the exercise. You can award points for every time someone gets one right and see who has the most points at the end. You can give three lives and after that they are eliminated or, as part of the three lives, you can go from both feet, to a knee to both knees when they make a mistake.

Through the gates (passing)

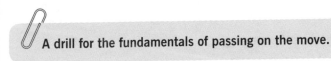

A drill for the fundamentals of passing on the move.

Objective

- To practise passing while moving in a confined space.

Resources

- 20 × 20m of space, one ball per pair and 8–30 cones (two per gate)

What to do

1. Set up a 20 × 20m grid. Place a series of gates (cones 1m apart) in it and have the group split into pairs.
2. Give the group three minutes to pass the ball through as many gates as possible in that time using the push pass (see page 32).
3. The main teaching point with this drill is ensuring your head is kept up, so that you are aware of what is around you in terms of people in your way, where the gates are and which gates are free.
4. The next teaching point is talking to each other so that as a pair you know where your partner is and where they are going.

```
A o o        o o    C    D D
A      B o o        o o
o o      B      o o C      o o
EE    o o    FF      o o
```

Figure 2.2 Football activities – through the gates (passing).

Variations

- A good alteration is to introduce new gates and take some out in order to ensure people keep their heads up to see where the gates are.
- Another change is to have some groups without a ball so that the pairs have to compete for a ball, as well as trying to pass through cones. This can be used for rugby, netball, basketball and hockey.

Line passing

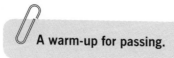

A warm-up for passing.

Objective

- To practise passing the ball quickly while still maintaining accuracy.

Resources

- One ball and two cones per group of six

What to do

1. Split everyone into groups of four (ensure there are an even number of groups). Combine two groups together to have a larger group of eight.
2. Set up two cones 4.5m apart for each group and have four people line up behind each cone.
3. The person at the front of the line passes to the person at the front of the opposite line and then runs to the back of the line they are in. The process continues.

Variation

- Again this can be used for all the invasion sports covered in this book. This can also be adapted for picking a ball up in rugby if the person at the front of line A rolls the ball for the person in the B line to pick up.

One v. one dribbling

Objective

- To develop dribbling past a defender.

Resources

- One ball and 5 × 10m of space per group of seven

What to do

1. Set up a series of 5 × 10m grids.
2. Have three people stand at either end of each grid with a person in the middle (defender).
3. The ball starts at one end of the grid with someone trying to dribble to the other end. Once they have made it, or have been tackled, the ball is passed to the opposite end (from which the first player started) and the next person will try to make it to the opposite end.
4. This is where the sport-specific dribbling skills should be used.
5. Ensure the defender is regularly swapped so that everyone gets a chance to practise.

Variations

- This can be used for football, basketball, hockey and rugby.
- To increase the challenge, add a time limit.
- Try using different numbers of attackers and defenders.

Basic shooting

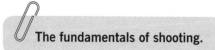

The fundamentals of shooting.

Objectives

- To improve shooting.
- To improve shooting with the laces.

Resources

- One ball and 5 × 10m of space per pair

What to do

1. Set up a series of 5m-wide goals. Then place cones 5m either side of the goal.
2. Have a goalkeeper who stands in the goal and then another person at each cone. The person with the ball then tries to shoot past the goalkeeper. The person at the other end will then get the ball and, once the goalkeeper has shouted 'ready', they will shoot. The process is then repeated.
3. Remember to swap everyone around so that everyone gets a chance to shoot; and ensure that people are trying to use the laces to shoot.
4. Encourage aiming low and into the corners as this is the hardest area for the goalkeeper to reach.

Figure 2.3 Football activities – basic shooting.

Variations

- This can be used for both hockey and football.
- If these are set up side by side you can have a ladder competition whereby a pair play against each other for three minutes. Whoever wins moves up into the next grid and whoever loses moves down into the grid below. You can devise your own way of deciphering who wins if it is a draw but ideas such as rock, paper, scissors work well.
- An alternative is to have three people behind each cone and start with a ball at each end, so after shooting everyone collects their ball and the other end can carry on.

World Cup heading

 A practical conditioned heading drill.

Objective

- To improve the accuracy of heading.

Resources

- One ball and 5 × 5m of space per group of four

What to do

1. Split the group into pairs, and set up a series of 5 × 5m grids. Each pair will join up with another pair and will have a grid to work in.
2. Each person kneels down along a different side of the square (ensuring their partner is not opposite them). There will be one ball per grid. Someone will start with the ball and, while staying on their knees, will throw the ball in the air and try to head it past someone from the other pair through the cones marking the side of the grid. Everyone will take turns at heading and the group as a whole must keep track of their score.
3. Swap the pairs around every three minutes so that the pairs play against as many people a possible.
4. The coaching point is to aim the header towards the corner and to really use the arms and neck to power forwards into the header and ideally, starting on their knees, they should end up falling towards the ground.

Variation

- This can be done on an individual basis so that you can head the ball in all three directions.

Figure 2.4 Football activities – World Cup heading.

Pass and shoot

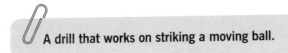

A drill that works on striking a moving ball.

Objective

- To improve striking a moving ball.

Resources

- One ball and 5 × 8m of space per group

What to do

1. Set up a series of 5m-wide goals and have a goalkeeper in each. Then have a cone in line with one of the posts about 3m out with a person standing by this cone with some balls, as they will be a server. Have an additional cone in line with the other post that is 3m further back.
2. The server passes to the other cone, the person at the front of the cue will run and strike the ball and try to score. They then collect their ball, give it back to the feeder and rejoin the back of the queue, by which time the next person will have gone and the process is repeated. It is important to ensure that when returning the ball they do not run across the grid; instead they must run around it.
3. Remember to regularly change the goalkeeper and feeders and try to use both a pass shot (inside of the foot) and a power shot (laces).

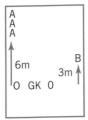
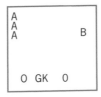

Figure 2.5 Football activities – pass and shoot.

Variations

- This can be used for both hockey and football.
- The position of the feeder can be changed to alongside and behind the striker and from side to side so as to work both feet.
- This can be used for basketball with the same set-up, just a basket rather than a goal and goalkeeper.
- This can be used for lay-ups and set shots.

Throw, head, catch

Putting heading and moving together in a game-like situation.

Objectives

- To be able to head the ball when moving.
- To develop spatial awareness.

Resources

- One ball

What to do

1. Split the group into two teams and make a grid 20 × 20m with a 5m-wide goal at opposite ends.
2. The game works by throwing or heading the ball rather than using your feet. The aim is to complete a sequence of throwing, heading and catching within your team. Every time a sequence is completed your team scores a point.
3. If you manage to throw the ball into the goal you also get a point, but if you head the ball into the goal you get five points.
4. You cannot throw the ball for yourself to head, or catch after you have headed the ball.

The technique of heading is important, as is the idea of finding space, and what you should tell the attacking group is to move to somewhere none of their teammates are. Also tell them that they may not always get the ball but by moving into space their team can keep the ball as defenders are likely to follow them.

NB The opposition can only catch the ball after a header.

Doctor, doctor

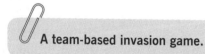

A team-based invasion game.

Objective

- To put into practice the teamworking and spatial awareness elements of invasion games.

Resources

- One ball per person and two bibs

What to do

1. Create a grid measuring up to 60 × 60m, with two 5 × 5m grids diagonally opposite each other.

2. Split the group into two teams. Each team must select a doctor who stands in one of the 5 × 5m grids. Everyone else has a ball.

3. Each player dribbles their ball around and tries to hit people on the opposing team between the knee and toe. If hit, you must sit where you are and wait for their doctor to come and set you free. To be set free the doctor has to tap you on the head (or high-five you).

4. The doctor cannot be hit while in their 5 × 5m grid, but if the doctor is hit outside their grid, again between the knee and the toe, then they too must sit on the floor, but, as they are their team's only doctor, then there is no one to set them or anyone else on their team free.

- For rugby or for general invasion have the players run around with a ball in their hands and use tag belts.
- If playing with a larger group you can have several doctors for each team.

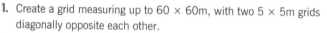

DOCTOR	A		B	A	B	A		B
A	B	A	B	A	B	A	B	
	B		B		B		DOCTOR	

Figure 2.6 Football activities – doctor, doctor.

Dribbling scrimmages

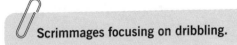

Scrimmages focusing on dribbling.

Objective

- To put dribbling into an actual game situation.

Resources

- One ball, enough bibs for half of the group, two goals and a large space

What to do

1. Set up a large pitch (as this allows more space to encourage dribbling), with goals/nets.
2. Every time somebody takes the ball past someone, they score a point. These are added to any points scored in the normal way.

Figure 2.7 Football activities – dribbling scrimmages.

Variations

- Set up zones on the pitch to create thirds. Any time someone dribbles into a more attacking third, they score a point.
- Another variation is to have the same zones, but with the rule that you cannot pass into a new zone, thereby ensuring dribbling has to happen.
- These can be used for football, hockey and basketball.

Chapter 3
Rugby

Holding a rugby ball

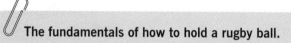

The fundamentals of how to hold a rugby ball.

Objective

- To introduce the basic and most effective method for holding a ball.

Resources

- One ball per group of six

What to do

1. The natural reaction when holding a rugby ball is to put the ball under one arm, but this is inefficient.
2. The most efficient way to hold a ball is in both hands (as you can then pass at any time and it is more secure). Place each hand on opposite panels (sides) of the ball so that the palms of the hands are opposite but so that the fingers run across onto the next panel. Once the fingers are in place the ball should then be held out in front of you about 13cm away from the body.
3. The reason this should be taught is that this is the basic preparation for a pass and also how the ball should be if you are picking it up off the ground or catching it.
4. A good way to practise basic handling is to have the group do activities such as passing the ball through their legs in a figure of eight formation or passing the ball around their waists.

Variation

- Another idea is to divide the group into teams of six and do things like over, under, or side to sides. Have each team in a line and the first person goes over their head and the next under their legs.

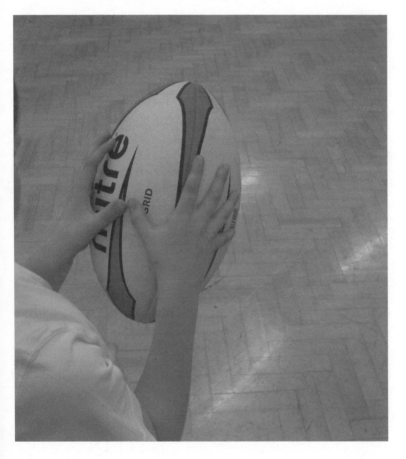

How to pick up a ball

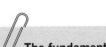 The fundamentals of how to pick up a ball from the ground.

Objective

- To introduce ways of picking up a ball that is on the ground when moving.

Resources

- One ball per pair and 20 × 20m of space

What to do

1. Practise this at walking pace first, before gradually increasing to a jog and finishing with running at full pace.
2. As the ball is on the floor, move towards it and place a foot 10cm to the side of the ball, ensuring that it points forwards. The other foot should be about shoulder width behind the first foot and pointing at a 90° angle away from the body.
3. Bend both knees and bring the hands down towards the ball. Pick up the ball with both hands (as with the basic grip), bring the back foot forwards and push the body upwards so that both legs and the back begin to straighten. This should be done in a similar way to a sprinter leaving the blocks and should therefore allow you to move away quickly.
4. Have the group inside a 20 × 20m grid with half with a ball and half without. As you say 'Down', those with a ball place it on the floor, for those without to then approach and pick up. Gradually increase the pace of approach and exits.

Variation

- Another method is to have the group in pairs and have them roll the ball to each other. Here you have to watch the ball carefully in order to account for the bounce. This is where having one foot to the side and one slightly behind comes in, as this should prevent the ball from moving past you.

Running lines

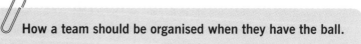

How a team should be organised when they have the ball.

Objective

- To introduce the idea of team lines in order to ensure that the ball can always be passed backwards.

Resources

- 5 × 10m of space and one ball per group of five

What to do

1. With the rule of not being able to pass the ball forwards comes the added complication of where to stand so as to ensure that you can always receive a pass. The answer is that you must always be behind the ball if you want it.

2. The most common method is to have a backwards-pointing diagonal line. The person with the ball should try to be in front of everyone else and if everyone is in a diagonal line this is easier.

3. Have the class in groups of five travelling down a 5 × 10m grid practising the diagonal line and passing the ball backwards while moving from one end to the other (see Figure 3.1).

4. The key is that you do not just pass the ball as soon as you have it. Instead you will have to move forwards before passing the ball and look around as this will enable you to pass left or right.

5. Try to include this in as many of the rugby drills and games as possible.

Figure 3.1 Rugby skills – running lines.

How to pass a ball

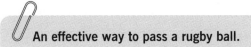

An effective way to pass a rugby ball.

Objective

- To introduce the basic technique for passing a rugby ball.

Resources

- One ball and 5 × 5m of space per pair

What to do

1. Hold the ball in both hands ensuring that the ball is just above waist height.
2. Place your left foot in the direction you want the ball to go. Bring the ball slightly towards the right-hand side of your body and then swing your hips and arms so that your body pivots to the left.
3. Release the ball just as it passes your hip but ensure that it is directed at the person you wish to pass to.
4. To pass to the right simply place the right foot in the direction you want to pass, take the ball towards the left-hand side and then swing through to the right and release the ball.
5. To begin with, practise this in pairs and have them simply hand the ball to each other using this technique and then gradually increase the distance between pairs. Practise this while stationary to begin with and then gradually allow the group to walk, then jog and finish with passing while running.

Variation

- As children become comfortable with the pass, encourage them to do it without moving their foot to point in the direction of the pass.

Tag rugby

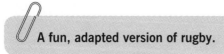

A fun, adapted version of rugby.

Objective

- To put rugby skills into practice.

Resources

- One rugby ball, bibs and tag belts

What to do

1. Set up a large area (around 20 × 30m) with a halfway line and two small areas that match the width of the pitch at either end.
2. Explain that some of the rules are the same as normal rugby in that you can only pass backwards and that offside means that you have to be behind the ball anytime play restarts.
3. Where tag rugby is different is that there is no contact (so tag belts are used) and kicking is not allowed.
4. Attackers try to score a try by putting the ball down (in a controlled manner) in the try area. Attackers can pass (backwards) and run with the ball. Defenders try to stop them.
5. If a defender grabs an attacker's belt when they have the ball, the defender stands with the belt held aloft. When this happens the teacher shouts 'tag', the attacker stops and passes to somebody on their team for play to resume. At this point defenders have to move behind the ball.
6. Start the game with a free pass. This is a pass from the halfway line which cannot be intercepted by the defending team. Use the free pass to restart play after a try has been scored or if possession changes due to the ball being knocked forward, thrown forward or if someone runs out of the pitch markings with the ball.

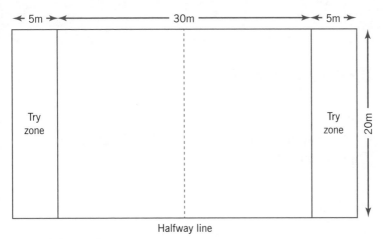

Halfway line

Figure 3.2 Rugby skills – tag rugby.

Variation

- Limit the number of touches in any attacking phase once the basic concepts have been understood.

Class, clap, catch

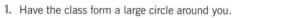 An enjoyable warm-up activity to practise catching and improve concentration.

Objectives

- To recap the fundamentals of catching a ball.
- To improve concentration.

Resources

- One ball

What to do

1. Have the class form a large circle around you.
2. Tell the group that if you throw the ball to them they must catch it.
3. After everyone has managed to catch the ball at least once, add the rule that, before they catch the ball, they must clap. However, if you dummy and they clap or they clap when the ball is not coming to them, they lose a life, just as they do if they drop the ball.
4. Everyone starts with three lives and if they lose the three lives they have to sit down.

Variations

- An alternative is just to award a point every time they get it right and deduct a point if they get it wrong.
- You can even use another adult and have two balls being used at the same time.

Catch me if you can

An enjoyable warm-up for evasive running.

Objective

- To get the class physically ready for the lesson ahead.

Resources

- 20 × 20m of space and at least one ball per pair

What to do

1. Set up a 20 × 20m grid and group the class into pairs.
2. The pairs number themselves 1 and 2. To begin, 1 runs around inside the grid trying to stay as far away from 2 as possible, while 2 tries to stay as close as possible to 1. After three minutes, reverse the roles.
3. Remind the group that they have to stay inside the grid and that, as well as looking for their partner, they must look around to ensure they don't bump into other people.
4. It is a good idea to swap the pairs around so that everyone gets to chase different people.
5. A good idea is to stop the group every 30 seconds to see how close the pairs are.
6. Whoever is being chased should be carrying a ball so that they get used to moving at speed with the ball.
7. If the group or pairs struggle with holding the ball and running, you can remove the ball. Alternatively, if the chaser is getting too close to their partner, you can give them a ball to make it slightly harder.

Stuck in the mud

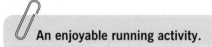

An enjoyable running activity.

Objectives

- To increase awareness of opponents when running.
- To improve changing direction.

Resources

- 20 × 20m of space, two bibs and one ball per person

What to do

1. Have everyone inside a 20 × 20m grid. Select two people to act as catchers and give everyone else a ball.
2. Those with a ball run around trying not to get tagged by the catchers. If they are tagged, they must stand still until set free by another person. (Rolling the ball through someone's legs is a good way to set someone free and works on picking up a ball as well, but this can be adapted to anything the group will appreciate.)
3. Regularly swap the catchers around so everybody gets a go and to prevent fatigue.

Variations

- This can be used for football, basketball, hockey and rugby.
- Alternatively, remove the ball and it can be used for Key Stage 1.

Traffic lights

The fundamentals of running with the ball.

Objective

- To improve the ability to stop or change direction on command.

Resources

- 20 × 20m of space and one ball per person

What to do

1. Everyone has a ball and runs around inside a 20 × 20m grid.
2. Tell the group that if you say 'Green', they must run quickly but when you say 'Red', they must stop as soon as they can and place the ball on the ground. (This works on the idea of close control as the ball always has to be within reaching distance so you can stop at any given point for football, hockey and basketball.)
3. After a while you can introduce the 'Orange', which is to change direction. The common problem with turning is collisions, so ensure you look behind to see what is there before actually turning.

Variations

- A good idea for advanced groups is to hold up red, green and orange items rather than saying the words as this encourages people to keep their heads up.
- This can be used for football, hockey and basketball following the above instructions.

Tidy your room

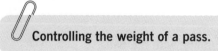

Controlling the weight of a pass.

Objectives

- To improve the time taken to pass.
- To improve the weighting of passes.

Resources

- 20 × 20m of space and at least one ball for every two children

What to do

1. Set up a 20 × 20m grid and then divide it into two connecting 10 × 20m grids. Split the group into two teams and have everyone with a ball.
2. The idea is to end with as few rugby balls on your side as possible. When you say go, the group passes balls from their half into the other teams' half. At the end of the time limit, five points are awarded for any balls that have landed in the other teams' 10 × 20m grid, but only one point for any that have landed outside the grid.
3. The teaching points to include are keeping your head up to see where the space is and where the balls are and controlling passes. Controlling the weighting of a pass is difficult to teach, so instead, the key is to allow them to practise in a trial and error manner.

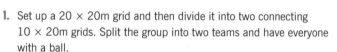

Figure 3.3 Rugby activities – tidy your room.

Variations

- This can be used for hockey, football, rugby, basketball, netball and fielding.
- For hockey and football the weight of the pass is proportional to the amount of back swing and degree of follow-through.
- For Key Stage 1, you can use non-sport-specific objects such as bean bags, as well as a variety of balls with no specific passing method.

British bulldogs

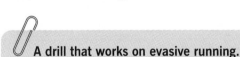

A drill that works on evasive running.

Objective

- To improve evasive movement in a restricted space.

Resources

- 20 × 20m of space, three bibs and one ball per person

What to do

1. Set up a 20 × 20m grid and select three people as catchers; then have everyone stand at an end with a ball.
2. The other three people do not have a ball and are catchers.
3. The aim of everyone with a ball is to make it from their end to the other without being tugged. You repeat until there is nobody left.

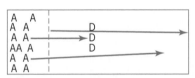

Figure 3.4 Rugby activities – British bulldogs.

Variation

- This can be used for football, basketball and hockey.

Breakaway

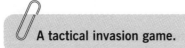

A tactical invasion game.

Objective

• To use teamwork in a game situation.

Resources

• 20 × 20m of space, three cones and three balls

What to do

1. Set up a 20 × 20m grid and place three cones slightly away from one end, as shown in Figure 3.5. Split the group into two teams with each team having an end for themselves.
2. Place a ball on each of the cones in the grid and have one team stand behind the end closest to them. This team will be the defending team. The other team will be at the opposite end and will be the attacking team.
3. The attacking team run out and try to get one of the balls from the cone back to their line by running with the ball. If they are tagged by a defender before making it back to their starting line, they are out and if a defender enters the grid but fails to catch anyone, then they are out.
4. If the attacker fails to get a ball then nothing happens.
5. The aim is to get all three balls back. After this they swap the roles. It is a good idea to have 3–4 swaps as the group will get increasingly used to the game and will begin to dummy and fake and think tactically.

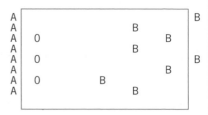

Figure 3.5 Rugby activities – breakaway.

Get and go

 An enjoyable teamworking game that works on moving with a ball.

Objective

- To practise picking up and running with the ball.

Resources

- As many rugby balls as possible

What to do

1. Set up three connected 10 × 20m grids, as shown in Figure 3.6 and split the class into two teams.
2. Each team starts in one of the end grids. The aim is to run into the opposition's grid, pick up a ball and bring it into their grid.
3. If someone drops the ball at any point they must leave it where it is and return back to their grid before they continue.
4. If you are holding a ball and are tagged by an opponent without a ball when in the middle grid, you must again leave the ball where it is and return to your grid.
5. The team with the most balls in their grid at the end are the winners.
6. Play several times to allow people to develop strategies.

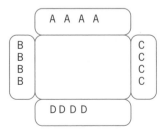

Figure 3.6 Rugby activities – get and go.

Variation

- A good variation is to have a middle grid of 10×10m but then have smaller grids of 5×10m attached to each side of the middle grid. This works on the basis of having four teams rather than two and therefore increases the need for tactical thinking. You must enter an opponent's grid through the middle section.

Chapter 4
Hockey

Holding a hockey stick

The basic grip for holding a hockey stick.

Objective

- To introduce the grip for holding a hockey stick.

Resources

- One hockey stick per person

What to do

1. The grip for holding a hockey stick is unusual in the sense that the grip is the same for both left- and right-handed people. It is essential to remember that only the flat face of the stick can be used to hit the ball.
2. The right hand should be placed approximately 30cm down the stick (this should be towards the bottom of the grip). The right hand is the support hand.
3. The left hand should be placed around the top of the stick and is the control hand as it dictates the movement and direction of the stick (much like the rudder on a boat). The thumb and index finger on both hands should create a 'V' shape.

Dribbling

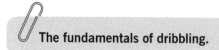

The fundamentals of dribbling.

Objective

- To introduce the fundamentals of dribbling.

Resources

- 20 × 20m of space and one stick and ball per person

What to do

1. Using the basic grip the aim is to keep the ball just in front of you so that it is always within reaching (playing) distance. This can be done either through keeping the ball in constant contact with the stick (for control) or by tapping the ball (for speed).
2. Keeping the ball at stick's length enables you to change direction or speed quickly and also allows you to pass or shoot. As you have these options it is important to keep your head up as much as possible to see which is the best option. This is best worked on once the control of the ball during dribbling has been mastered.
3. To begin with, have the group inside a 20 × 20m grid with everyone dribbling and trying to avoid each other.

The push

The basic technique for passing in hockey.

Objective

- To introduce the basic push pass used for passing a hockey ball accurately.

Resources

- One ball and 5 × 5m of space per pair and one stick per person

What to do

1. The push pass is used for passing the ball over short distances. It is easy to do and very accurate.
2. Your left foot should be pointed forward in the direction you want the ball to travel. The right foot should be placed in line with the left foot but slightly wider than shoulder width behind it and positioned to create a 90° angle between your feet.
3. The ball should be in line with the right foot. Place the stick so that the flat face is in contact with the ball and then slant the stick so that your right hand is in line with the middle of the gap between your legs. Both knees should be bent with your weight being on your back (right) leg. Your body position will be low at the start but will end with you being upright.

4. Keep the stick in contact with the ball and slide it by pulling back with your left hand and pushing forward with your right hand, until it is in line with the middle of your left foot. Ensure that you are always watching the ball (the longer the stick is in contact with the ball the more powerful the pass will be). At this point your weight should shift onto the front (left) foot and the stick should be brought into the air so that it is no longer in contact with the ball. As you slide the stick through, take a small step with your right foot so that it is again facing the direction you want the ball to travel in and if you continue to watch the ball then your head and the momentum of the slide should bring your body back upright so that you can continue to play.

5. This is best practised by having the group in pairs 5m apart and passing back and forth. As the group progresses you can get them to move further apart or pass to each other while moving.

Control

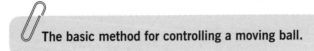

The basic method for controlling a moving ball.

Objective

- To introduce the basic technique for stopping a ball.

Resources

- One ball and 5 × 5m of space per pair and one stick per pair

What to do

1. The most important part of controlling a moving ball is judging the path of the ball and getting yourself into position. Watch the ball and decide where the ball is going to pass by you. Place your left foot pointing in the direction the ball is coming from and 15cm parallel to the left-hand side of where you think the ball will pass you. The right foot should be placed about shoulder width behind the left foot and positioned so that it is where you want the ball to stop. (This is the same foot positioning as the push pass.)

2. Have your stick slightly slanted and placed on the ground in line with the right foot and positioned exactly where you think the ball will go. Both knees should be slightly bent. Getting the stick in position as early as possible is beneficial as it allows you more time to get the rest of your body in position.

3. Your grip should be 'normal' in the sense that it is not a firm grip (as the ball would just bounce off) and not too relaxed (as the ball wouldn't stop). This is commonly referred to as 'soft hands' across sport.

4. As the ball approaches, bend your knees even more and as the ball hits the stick you are looking to cushion it, so that you bring the stick about 5cm back while keeping the ball in contact with the head of the stick.

5. This is best practised in the same way as the push pass and it is recommended that you teach the push pass and then the control as you can use the same set-up. The main aim of the control is to be able to play the ball as soon as possible, so putting the two together allows you to see how your control affects the time it takes you to pass.

The hit

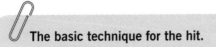

The basic technique for the hit.

Objective

- To introduce the basic hit.

Resources

- One ball and 5 × 5m of space per pair and one stick per person

What to do

1. This is used mainly for shooting but can also be used for passing over a long distance. The first thing to do is bring your right hand up the stick so that it is next to the left hand.
2. The left foot should be pointed forward in the direction you want the ball to travel. The right foot should be in line with left foot but shoulder width behind and positioned to create a 90° angle between your feet.
3. The ball should be to the right-hand side of the right foot, just short of an arm's length away (so that the swing of the hockey stick doesn't have to be adjusted).
4. Then bring the stick back into the air (but remember the stick head cannot go above waist height), shifting your body weight onto the back (right) foot and then swing the stick through so that it connects with the ball. At this point the weight should be evenly balanced between both legs. As the stick connects with the ball you should be looking down at the ball.
5. It is important to follow through as this adds more power (but again be careful the stick head doesn't rise above waist height), and as the ball is struck your eyes should follow the ball to bring the head back up to a normal position. As you follow through your weight should be transferred onto the left foot so that your momentum takes you forwards.

6. Have the group in pairs in 5m grids, with a person at either end to create two goals. First have them trying to aim the hit at the middle of the goal, then as the group progresses you can change the aim so that they are trying to score past each other or you can increase the distance between the two goals.

Block tackle

The fundamentals of tackling.

Objective

- To introduce the fundamentals of the block tackle.

Resources

- One ball and 5 × 10m of space per pair and one stick per person

What to do

1. Tackling in hockey is a very difficult skill. As the attacker approaches you it is important not to lunge in for the ball. Set your body position so that your left foot is pointing in the direction the attacker is coming from and just to the side of where you think the attacker will pass you. The right foot should be placed shoulder width behind the left foot. It is essential to remain light on your feet (not flat-footed) as you may have to change direction quickly. Both knees should also be slightly bent.
2. Timing is crucial because if you put your stick down too early you will become immobile and it will be easy for your opponent to dribble around you, yet if you put the stick down too late they will have already passed you or you will foul them. Therefore have your stick at your side so that the stick head is at knee height, ready to be put on the ground.
3. As the attacker is about a metre in front of you, put the stick on the ground just in front of where the ball is and move your right foot so that it is behind the stick (as this adds more weight and therefore strength to the tackle). Have a firm grip as you have to stop the momentum of the ball and change its direction.
4. The attacker should then be past you, but the ball should remain in contact with your stick. You should quickly decide what you are going to do, whether that is dribbling or passing because if you simply stand still the attacker will turn and try to tackle you.

5. Have the group in pairs with a ball in 5 × 10m channels and have one as the attacker and one as the defender and see if the defender can stop the attacker reaching the other end using the techniques above.

6. When tackling on the move, it is important to judge how fast to travel on the approach towards the attacker as, if you sprint towards them, you could be caught flat-footed, but if you are too slow in approaching them, they can pass or shoot. Instead you should sprint so that you are about 5m away from the attacker and then get yourself quickly into position to tackle as described above. If it takes you longer to get into position, this distance will have to be increased.

Hook turn

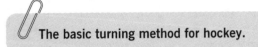

The basic turning method for hockey.

Objective

* To introduce the basic hook turn.

Resources

* 20 × 20m of space and one ball and stick per person

What to do

1. Dribble the ball as usual. Move the ball so it is just ahead of your left foot.
2. Bring your left foot so it is in line with the ball but approximately 10cm to the right-hand side.
3. Keep your stick in contact with the ball.
4. Bring your right foot around so that it creates a 90° angle between your feet. Then twist your body around, push the ball forwards and accelerate away in the opposite direction to which you started.
5. Have everyone dribbling around inside a 20 × 20m grid, practising the turn. As children become comfortable introduce defenders so that dribblers have to avoid them.

Through the gates (dribbling)

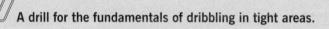

A drill for the fundamentals of dribbling in tight areas.

Objective

- To practise dribbling when space is limited.

Resources

- 20 × 20m of space, 8–30 cones (to create gates) and one stick and ball per person

What to do

1. Set up a 20 × 20m grid, place a series of gates (two cones, 1m apart) and make sure everyone has a stick and ball.
2. Give the group three minutes to dribble through as many gates as possible.
3. The main teaching point with this drill is ensuring the head is kept up so that you can be aware of what is around you in terms of people in your way, where the gates are and which gates are free.
4. The next teaching point is keeping the ball close to you so that as people approach or you notice a free gate you can change direction quickly to travel through it.

Variations

- A good alteration to make is to introduce new gates and take some out in order to ensure people keep their heads up to see where the gates are.
- Another change is to remove some of the balls so that teams have to compete for a ball as well as trying to dribble through cones. This can be used for football, rugby, basketball and hockey.

Round, through, me and you

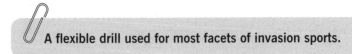

A flexible drill used for most facets of invasion sports.

Objective

- To put the skills and techniques learnt into a game-related situation.

Resources

- 20 × 20m of space, one stick per person and one ball

What to do

1. Split the group into two teams and have a team either side of a 20 × 20m grid, with goals on the other sides of the grid.
2. To begin with, when you say 'Go', the people at the front of both lines will run left, around the furthest goal and into the grid, by which time you will have put a ball into the middle. They then have to compete for the ball and try to dribble past their opponent and score, just as they would in a game.
3. After a while, give everyone a number just to keep them guessing as to who is next. This is where the fundamentals of dribbling and shooting will be tested.
4. Another idea is to have more than one person from each side go, so that they have to work as a team, meaning the passing element is also present.

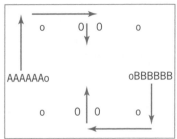

Figure 4.1 Hockey activities – round, through, me and you.

Variations

- This can be used as a dribbling drill for hockey, football and basketball (use a hoop on the floor as the target).
- As a passing drill, this can then also be used for netball (again, a target rather than a net) and for rugby (on a tag basis).

Three-team turnaround

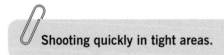

Shooting quickly in tight areas.

Objective

* To put the technique of shooting into a game-related situation.

Resources

* 20 × 20m of space, six bibs, one stick per person and six balls

What to do

1. Select a goalkeeper and then split the rest of the group into three teams. Set a grid 20m in length and width. Have a team scattered around the outside, with a ball by their stick, and the other teams in the middle with one team wearing bibs.
2. The team members on the outside are given individual numbers and any time their number is called they then pass their ball into the grid for the others to play within a six v. six game. Once the ball leaves the grid or a goal is scored a new number will be called until all of the balls have gone.
3. Then the team on the outside switches places with a team on the inside and the game continues as before.
4. To begin with, line the people up on the outside in numerical order, but after a while change the numbers around so that everyone has to look up to see where the new ball is coming from.

Figure 4.2 Hockey activities – three-team turnaround.

Variations

- This can be used for football, hockey, basketball and netball. If using the drill for netball or basketball, there is no need for a goalkeeper and it is the net rather than goal.
- This can be played without goalkeepers if no one wants to go in goal or if the class size favours omitting a goalkeeper.

Passing scrimmages

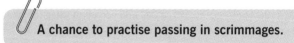

A chance to practise passing in scrimmages.

Objective

- To put the passing skills taught into a game situation.

Resources

- A large space, one ball, one bib for every two children and one stick per person

What to do

1. Set a normal-sized pitch or court (this will depend on the age and size of the group, but adjust to fit).
2. There are a variety of ideas to use. Splitting the area into zones and not allowing people to move out of zones forces the group to pass.
3. Another idea is to say that, before a goal can be scored, five passes need to be made or that everyone has to have a touch before a goal can be scored.
4. Another option is to say that if five passes are made that team gets a point or use this as the sole means of scoring so that there are no goals.

A		AB	B	
GK B	AB		A GK	
A		AB	B	

Figure 4.3 Hockey activities – passing scrimmages.

Variation

- These ideas work across football, hockey, basketball and netball.

Chapter 5
Netball

Two-handed catch

The fundamentals of catching a ball.

Objective

- To introduce the two-handed pass.

Resources

- One ball and 5 × 5m of space per pair

What to do

1. It is essential to watch the ball throughout the skill, especially as the ball is passed to you. As you watch the ball in flight ensure you are in line with the ball's path.
2. Once in line with the ball, prepare yourself to receive the ball by having your feet shoulder width apart with both feet pointing forwards. Have both hands out in front of your chest with your fingers spread and your thumbs close together to form a 'W' shape.
3. As the ball approaches you, step forward and reach towards the ball. As the ball enters your hands cup your fingers around the ball and bring your hands back towards your chest by bending your arms. (This means the ball will be in position for you to then be able to play the ball without having to adjust your body position too much.)
4. This is best taught straight after you have taught the two-handed pass (see page 120) and uses the same set-up of having the group in pairs 5m apart. The advantage of this is that it allows the group to see how important the catch is for their next move. As the group progresses you can increase the distance between the pairs.

Variation

- This can also be used and practised in the same way for basketball.

Bounce pass

A pass to move the ball beyond a close defender to a team-mate.

Objective

- To introduce the bounce pass.

Resources

- One ball and 5 × 5m of space per pair

What to do

1. The bounce pass is used to pass the ball under the arms of a close defender. Stand with both feet facing forwards, hold the ball in both hands with your fingers spread out and thumbs close together to form a 'W' shape around the ball. Hold the ball between hip and waist height straight in front of you.
2. Bend both knees and extend your arms as you push the ball forwards in the direction you want the ball to go. Aim for the ball to bounce about ⅔ of the distance between you and the person you are passing to so that the ball bounces up into their hands.
3. As you follow through, your fingers should end up pointing in the direction the ball has travelled.
4. Have the group in pairs 5m apart and passing to each other. Then introduce a defender as an obstacle for the attackers. Have the defender start off as static and gradually increase their movement.

Variations

- The pass is used in the same way in basketball.
- For the more advanced in the group you can introduce the one-handed bounce pass, which works on the same model but the ball is moved into one hand (as with the shoulder pass) to your side and then passed from there.

Pivoting

The technique for performing the pivot.

Objective

- To introduce the basic technique for pivoting with the ball.

Resources

- One ball and 5 × 10m of space per group

What to do

1. In netball, once you have the ball in your hands, the landing foot has to stay in contact with the ground. The pivot allows you to change direction without giving away a free pass.
2. If you have just landed (after jumping or stepping), then it is the landing foot that you pivot on. If both feet are on the floor when you receive the ball, then choose which foot is to become the landing foot.
3. Before you pivot ensure that the ball is held in both hands and close to your body (where it remains until the pivot is complete).
4. Bend both knees slightly and move onto the ball of the landing foot. You have to push off from the other foot to propel your body round to face the direction you desire. Ensure that both feet are firmly on the ground and your balance is set before trying to pass the ball.
5. With the class in groups of three, have each group in a straight line with 5m between each person. As the ball is passed into the middle, the person who receives the ball has to pivot and pass to the other end. Regularly swap positions to ensure that everyone get to practise the pivot. This can be used for basketball as well.

Shoulder pass

 The fundamentals of the shoulder pass.

Objective

- To introduce the shoulder pass.

Resources

- One ball and 5 × 5m of space per pair

What to do

1. The shoulder pass is used for passing over defenders.
2. Start by standing side-on, with your feet shoulder width apart and your left foot pointing forwards to create a 90° angle. At this stage both knees should be bent with your body weight over your back leg. The ball should be in both hands.
3. Bring the ball back to your right shoulder (using both hands), then remove the left hand so that the ball is in the palm of your right hand with the thumb and fingers spread around the back of the ball and use the left arm to maintain balance.
4. Take a small step to move the left foot further forwards but keep the right foot still. At the same time extend the right arm to push the ball forwards. This push should come from the fingers, wrist, elbow and shoulder.
5. Follow through so that the arm is fully extended and your fingers point along the path the ball has taken.
6. To begin with, have the group in pairs 5m apart passing back and forth. Then introduce a defender into the group so that they have to pass over the defender. To begin with the defender should be static but gradually increase the movement of the defender so that you end up with a 'piggy in the middle' type activity.

Variation

- This is a skill that is used in the exact same way for basketball.

Shooting

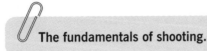

The fundamentals of shooting.

Objective

- To introduce the basic shooting technique for netball.

Resources

- One ball, one hoop and 5 × 5m of space per group

What to do

1. Start with your feet shoulder width apart so that you are balanced and positioned with your body and feet facing the post. Take the ball in your stronger hand and angle the wrist backwards slightly so that only the fingertips and thumb are in contact with the ball. The other hand should be placed gently on the side of the ball to help keep the ball balanced.
2. Hold the ball just above your head and bend your knees. Push from the knees and extend the shooting arm, upwards, then release the ball. A common problem is to aim for the ring, which results in not being able to get the ball up and over. Instead, you should aim for just above the ring to ensure that the ball clears it.
3. To begin with, have the group in pairs 5m apart just practising the technique. Then get one partner to hold their arms out in front of them to create a ring as the other shoots. For the next step you could have the group split into pairs or trios with a hoop being held horizontally in the air to create a more realistic target.
4. The final practice is to actually use a post and ring.

Throwing catch

 An enjoyable, teamworking version of tig.

Objective

- To practise throwing and catching, teamworking and movement.

Resources

- 20 × 20m of space and one ball

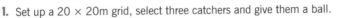

What to do

1. Set up a 20 × 20m grid, select three catchers and give them a ball.
2. Everyone else runs around inside the grid trying to avoid getting caught. If caught, they join the catchers.
3. The catching element is where the variation comes in. To be caught you have to be tagged by the ball. The catchers cannot move when they are holding the ball so they have to pass and move just as they would in a netball match.
4. Play the game until everyone has been caught.
5. Encourage the catchers to use everyone in order to catch people and to develop strategies for catching.

Netball stations

An enjoyable activity that works on a variety of core skills.

Objective

- To practise ball control, reactions and passing.

Resources

- One ball per person

What to do

1. Set up the eight stations, split the class into pairs and give everyone a ball.
2. Each pair has five minutes at each station but there may be several pairs at each station.
3. The stations are as follows.
   - Moving the ball around your legs in a figure of eight formation.
   - Moving the ball around your waist.
   - Stand back to back with your partner and, using one ball, pass it round to your partner, who will then pass it back.
   - Stand 5m apart, passing the ball with your partner.
   - Take the ball in one hand and pass it over your head into the opposite hand and then repeat.
   - Take it in turns to be the catcher and the dropper. The catcher bends down (as if to try to touch their toes) and looks at the ground. The dropper then drops the ball (from their chest height) and the catcher has to react and catch the ball before it hits the ground.
   - Partners stand 5m apart and one person throws the ball high, the other throws the ball low.
4. Where the tasks are individual, the partners compete against each other, but where it is a pair task, they compete against other pairs. The second time around the circuit, they can try to improve on their last score.

Keep your feet dry

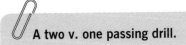

A two v. one passing drill.

Objective

- To improve passing and moving skills.

Resources

- One ball and 5 × 4m of space per group.

What to do

1. Set up a series of 5 × 4m grids and split the class into groups of three.
2. Each group has its own grid.
3. The grid is split so that there is a middle section (the river) of 2 × 5m and two end sections (riverbanks) of 1 × 5m. There should be 1 person in each section and the ball starts with a person in either of the end sections.
4. The aim is to pass the ball to the person on the other riverbank five times each without it being intercepted by the person in the river.
5. If the ball is intercepted, then the thrower swaps places with the person in the river and gets their feet wet. The idea is that you keep your feet dry by passing accurately.
6. Encourage the group to use a range of passes and to move around along the bank so that they can receive the ball.

Three square

A passing and moving warm-up.

Objectives

- To practise passing.
- To develop an understanding of moving to create space.

Resources

- 5 × 5m of space and one ball per group of three

What to do

1. Set up a series of 5 × 5m grids and split the class into groups of three.
2. Someone stands on the top corner, as shown below left, with the ball. The other two in the group have to ensure that they are on corners nearest to the ball to create the biggest angle for a pass.
3. The person with the ball then passes to whichever person they want to.
4. As the ball has moved, the other two people then need to move to recreate the wide angle, as shown below right.
5. This also helps the group to identify with creating space when in a game situation.

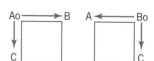

Figure 5.1 Netball activities – three square.

Variation

- Add a defender into the group to see if the three can keep the ball away from them.

Quick line

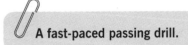

A fast-paced passing drill.

Objectives

- To practise the passing technique.
- To introduce passing on the move.

Resources

- One ball per group of eight

What to do

1. Set up eight cones in a zigzag shape and replicate for each group.
2. Have someone stand by each cone.
3. The ball starts at the first cone and is passed (using a chest pass) to the next person in the chain.
4. When the ball reaches the person at the end, the direction of the passes changes so that the ball finishes where it started.
5. The aim is to complete three full sets as quickly as possible. This will naturally lead to the different groups competing with each other.
6. Once the basic set-up has been mastered, double the number of cones for each group. Once someone has passed the ball, they have to move to the next free cone. Again, the aim is to complete three sets as quickly as possible. This now works on passing *and* moving.

Variation

- This can be used for all types of netball passes and the set-up also allows for its use for football, hockey and basketball.

Three v. one passing

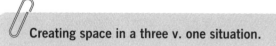

Creating space in a three v. one situation.

Objective

- To improve ball retention and passing technique.

Resources

- One ball, one bib and 5 × 5m of space per group

What to do

1. Set up a series of 5 × 5m grids and split the group into groups of three, each group having its own grid and ball.
2. To begin with, have the three just pass and move within the grid. After a while, change the groups so that there are four in each square. Give one person in each grid a bib and tell them they are a defender and the others have to try and keep the ball away from them.
3. It will be important to recap the technique for passing and catching the ball, but in terms of the possession element, the main coaching point will be ensuring that they can create and maintain a triangle. So if the ball is in corner 1 (see Figure 5.2), the other two attackers should be in corners 2 and 3. A good analogy to use is the idea of eating a pizza. If you have a narrow slice (small triangle), it is easy to eat, whereas a big slice (big triangle, corners 1, 2 and 3) would be difficult to eat, therefore, when narrow, the defender can 'gobble you up'.
4. As the ball moves, the attackers will have to move in order to maintain the big triangle.
5. Keeping the extra grids free allows for more space if a ball is passed out of a grid and gives good observation points for you.

Figure 5.2 Netball activities – three v. one passing.

Variations

- This can be used as explained for hockey, football, basketball and netball or as a basic handling drill for rugby.
- This can also be progressed into a six v. two or even any combination of team sizes in order to work on creating and maintaining space.

Robin Hood

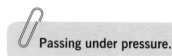

Passing under pressure.

Objective

- To practise passing with emphasis on speed.

Resources

- 10 × 10m of space, one ball per person and four cones

What to do

1. The corners of a 10 × 10m grid are marked out. The group is split into four groups, with each group placed in a line behind their designated corner. All of the available balls are placed in the middle.
2. The first person from each group runs into the middle, then passes the ball back to their group. Once at the corner the next person can go, and this continues until there are no balls left. To begin with, the team with the most balls at the end is the winner.
3. If anyone runs with the ball or more than one person from the group goes, then their balls must be put back into the middle.
4. Replay the game, but this time, after all of the balls from the middle have gone, the groups can take balls from other groups. It should still be one person from each group that is out fetching balls and everyone should get a turn. If someone does try to take a ball, no one is allowed to stop them.

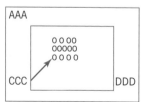

Figure 5.3 Netball activities – Robin Hood.

Variations

- This can be used for basketball, hockey, football and rugby, but would require a 20 × 20m grid.
- As a change for dribbling sports, allow people to dribble rather than having to pass the ball back to their group.
- When allowing the groups to take from each other you can use a key system, everyone starts with a key (cone) that they then trade for a ball.

Chapter 6
Basketball

Dribbling

 The basic technique for dribbling a basketball.

Objective

- To introduce the basic basketball dribble.

Resources

- 20 × 20m of space and one ball per person

What to do

1. The dribble in basketball is the most fundamental skill. It is important when you are dribbling that you do not catch the ball in two hands and then dribble again as this is against the rules (as it is travelling).
2. The dribble is just bouncing the ball by continuously and firmly pushing the ball towards the ground but angled slightly in front of you so that you can move forwards. As you bounce the ball, your fingers should be spread over the top of the ball. The aim is to have the ball bounce back up to hip height at every bounce.
3. As the ball bounces back up, your aim is to absorb the impact of it. This is done by keeping your hand on the ball until it reaches waist height, at which point you then bounce the ball downwards and forwards again. As you bounce the ball you should lean forwards so that your upper body is over it as this gives you greater control and helps shield the ball from defenders.

4. To begin with, have the group stand still and just practise bouncing the ball in front of them. Then allow them to move around a 20 × 20m grid, ensuring they avoid contact with anyone else. Gradually increase the speed at which they are moving around to finish with a full-paced dribble.

5. If a child struggles with the skill, sit them on the floor to practise dribbling and then gradually move to kneeling, kneeling on one knee and then standing still.

Two-handed pass

The fundamentals of the basic pass for basketball.

Objective

- To introduce the two-handed pass.

Resources

- One ball and 5 × 5m of space per pair

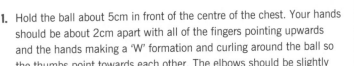

What to do

1. Hold the ball about 5cm in front of the centre of the chest. Your hands should be about 2cm apart with all of the fingers pointing upwards and the hands making a 'W' formation and curling around the ball so the thumbs point towards each other. The elbows should be slightly behind the body so that the ball can be held comfortably in this formation.
2. Then step forward onto either foot, pointing this foot in the direction you want the ball to travel, and push the arms away from the body in a forward and straight motion.
3. As you release the ball, continue to straighten the arms and push right through to the tips of the fingers. This controls the strength of the throw, which will determine how far you can pass the ball and is something the individual will pick up with practice. The aim for this pass is for it not to bounce before reaching the target and for the ball to reach your team-mate at chest height.
4. Have the class in pairs inside 5 × 5m grids practising passing to each other.

Variation

- This can be used for netball as well.

Two-handed shot

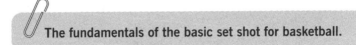

The fundamentals of the basic set shot for basketball.

Objective

• To introduce the two-handed shot.

Resources

• One ball, one basket with backboard and 5 × 5m of space per pair

What to do

1. Take the ball in both hands, so that your stronger hand is in the centre at the back of the ball. (This hand is the action hand.) Then angle your wrist backwards and aim it towards the basket. Your other hand plays a supporting role and should be positioned so that the fingertips are on the middle of the side of the ball. Your feet should be shoulder width apart and the foot on the same side as your action hand should be slightly ahead of the other foot.
2. Extend the action arm so that it straightens and, as you do so, lean forwards and bring your body to an upright position. (You are looking to reach as far as possible, so ideally you will end up on your tiptoes. A good teaching idea is to tell the group to reach to the sky.)
3. The aim is to loop the ball over the rim and into the basket. To begin with, it is best to aim for the backboard.

Variation

- The basic technique can be practised by having the group in pairs with someone of a similar height. Have the partners standing 5m apart. One has the ball and the other has their arms out in front of them to create a hoop. The one with the ball aims to shoot the ball through the hoop that is created. This emphasises the need for the ball to loop into the basket. This could be progressed to having hoops held in the air horizontally in pairs or groups of three, before finally introducing the basket.

The lay-up

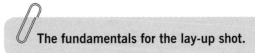

The fundamentals for the lay-up shot.

Objective

- To introduce the lay-up.

Resources

- One ball and 5 × 5m of space per pair

What to do

1. The lay-up shot appears to be very technical, but once grasped it is easy to execute, even in a game situation.
2. Dribble towards the net at an angle (as when you dribble straight it is difficult to get the ball over the rim).
3. When you are approximately 2m away from the net, take the ball in both hands and step forward (if right-handed this should be your left foot). As you step forward, bend your knee and move all of your weight onto this leg.
4. The next step is the actual leap. You should really power off from the front leg to allow you to jump as high as possible. As you are in the air you need to move the ball into your preferred hand. When you are at your highest point you need to roll (not throw) the ball towards the net. The roll should be soft and ideally off the backboard so it lands in the basket.
5. You should aim to land on both feet as this is safest.
6. To begin with, have the group in pairs just practising the dribble and jump, then ask them to roll the ball to their partner as they jump. Finally, introduce the basket and have the group practise the skill in its entirety.

Ball manipulation

 Simple activities to increase ball familiarisation.

Objective

- To develop ball familiarisation.

Resources

- One ball per two children

What to do

1. Split the class into pairs and give each pair a ball.
2. Introduce a variety of small activities, giving each person 30 seconds to practise or one minute for joint activities.
3. The activities are:
   - Passing the ball around your body (left to right and right to left)
   - Passing the ball around one leg (alternate legs)
   - Passing the ball through your legs (figure of eight in both directions)
   - Bouncing the ball
   - **Joint:** back to back passing in either direction
   - **Joint:** back to back passing either overhead or through the legs.

Variation

- The joint activities can be done as races in larger teams.

Ten times rhyme

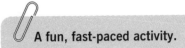

A fun, fast-paced activity.

Objective

- To explore a range of movements.

What to do

1. Have everybody inside a large area.
2. The activity uses a number of saying and corresponding actions. To begin with introduce them one or two at a time and progress through them at a pace which suits your group. You could even spread it out over a number of lessons and build the excitement about learning the next part, next lesson.
3. Every time you say a number, the group must shout out the rhyme and then perform the action. It is vital that you are enthusiastic and energetic to help generate the pace needed.
   - 1 is 'on the run', so they dribble around inside the space
   - 2 is 'on my shoe', so they put their foot on the ball
   - 3 is 'on my knee', so they put their knee on the ball
   - 4 is 'on the floor', so they lie down
   - 5 is 'staying alive', so they sing and dance to the song 'Staying Alive'
   - 6 is 'show some tricks', so children do any action they can think of with the ball
   - 7 is 'point to heaven', so they point up at the sky
   - 8 is 'find a mate', so they have to find a partner as quickly as possible
   - 9 is 'on the line', so they have to get to wherever you are as quickly as possible
   - 10 is 'do it all again', so you go through 1–9 really quickly.

Variations

- You and the class will be able to think of alternatives for each of the numbers and that is very much encouraged.
- The activity can also be used for Key Stage 1, with the minor adjustment of not using a ball.

King of the ring

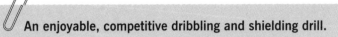

An enjoyable, competitive dribbling and shielding drill.

Objective

- To improve close control and ball manipulation.

Resources

- 20 × 20m of space and one ball per person

What to do

1. Everyone is in a 20 × 20m grid with a ball.
2. Everyone then attempts to knock other people's balls out of the grid while ensuring their own ball stays in.
3. Once your ball is knocked out, you are eliminated and wait on the side, practising skills.

Variations

- This can be used for basketball, football and hockey. Give each person three lives. Use the people on the outside as defenders so give them the chance to go in and try to eliminate someone and then come back out.
- A good variation is, once eliminated, you get five seconds to get someone else's ball. If after five seconds, you have a ball under control, you continue with that; if not, you are out. If you get someone else's ball, they are out and will then get five seconds themselves. It is important that students come to you once out so you can control the five-second rule.
- If the group is advanced, you can have pairs so there is one ball between two but work with the same rules.

Endball

A fun, game-related activity.

Objective

- To put the techniques and skills learnt so far into practice.

Resources

- 30 × 20m of space and one ball

What to do

1. Split the group into two teams and create a grid 20 × 20m with a 5 × 20m extension at opposite ends.
2. Select a person from each team and place them in the extended area of the grid and, although they can move around, they must stay within the area.
3. The teams play as if in a normal game but, rather than scoring through a net, they have to pass to the person in the end zone.

A		B		AB		A			B
	B	A		AB		B	A		
		B		AB		A			

Figure 6.1 Basketball activities – endball.

Variations

- You can place more than one person in the end zone, or even attackers and defenders in the end zone.
- This can be played as a game for any invasion game with the sport-specific rules.
- To make this a rugby game, you can either play it as a basic throwing and catching game or say the ball cannot go forwards unless passing to the end zone.

Jail break

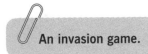

An invasion game.

Objective

- To practise teamwork and spatial awareness.

Resources

- A large space, one bib for every two children and one ball per person

What to do

1. Split the group into two teams. Set up a large grid (up to around 60 × 60m but smaller can be used) with a halfway line. The halfway line signifies each team's half. Within each half, place two small grids 5 × 5m in the furthest corners. Place balls in diagonally opposite grids, as shown in Figure 6.2.
2. The aim is to run from your half into the opposition's and get a ball and dribble it back into your own half and put it in your ball grid. However, when you are in the opposition's grid, if you are tagged by one of them (with or without the ball), you have to go into the jail, which is the other grid in the opposition's half.
3. You can be set free by someone running into the opposition's half and into the jail. If you make it to the jail, then you are free to take someone from the jail back to your half to set them free. (You cannot be tagged once you have made it to the jail but you must head straight back to your half.)
4. If at any time you shout 'jailbreak', then everyone in the jail is set free. When coming out of jail, you have to go back to your own half before you can go and get a ball.

5. The team with the most balls at the end wins.

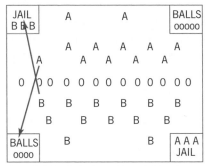

Figure 6.2 Basketball activities – jail break.

Variations

- This can be done on the basis of picking up a ball, kicking a ball or dribbling a ball, depending on if you want this to be sport-specific.
- You can even use general objects such as bean bags to make this a general invasion game.

Introduction

The technical elements of net/wall and striking and fielding games can be very difficult to teach, but obviously without the basic techniques the games fail. The basic techniques are therefore provided in a lot of detail and the best thing to do is to ensure you physically practise them yourself before the lesson. When teaching the basic skills, teach them part by part and do not sacrifice perfecting the skill for the sake of progressing the lesson quickly.

With the technical emphasis it is important that when you use game and game-related activities you try to make them as fun as possible. Do not overload the group with rules as PE needs to be both educational and enjoyable.

This section is easily adapted to suit indoor PE as well through using plastic and foam equipment. Another good teaching idea for indoor PE is to use masking tape to mark out grids as it provides a physical line (which is difficult to achieve with cones) that doesn't move, but is easily removed at the end of the lesson.

Chapter 7
Striking and fielding

Catching

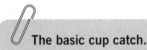

The basic cup catch.

Objective

- To introduce the basic cup catch technique.

Resources

- One ball and 5 × 5m of space per pair

What to do

1. As the ball is travelling towards you, move into the ball's path. Cup your hands together so that the little fingers are together.
2. The hands should be placed so that they are approximately 7–8 cm in front of the middle of the torso. Some people may find it more natural to cup the hands at hip height, so allow whichever feels comfortable.
3. Both the hands and arms should be relaxed at this point.
4. As the ball enters your hands, close your fingers around the ball and bring your hands in close to your body.
5. The best way to practise this is in pairs, throwing the ball back and forth with a partner. Alternatively, have everyone walking around on their own throwing the ball in the air and catching it.

Variations

- You can have the partners moving around as they throw to each other.

- An alternative is to have groups of four and have no set order of who throws to whom. This means the ball will come from different directions and you will be able to explain the importance of having the hands out ready for a catch and always watching the ball.
- You can also explain how bouncing on your toes helps you to be ready as it ensures you are not flat-footed.

The long barrier

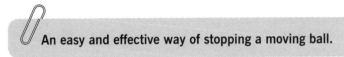

An easy and effective way of stopping a moving ball.

Objective

- To introduce the skill of the long barrier.

Resources

- One ball and 5 × 5m of space per pair

What to do

1. Watch the ball as it moves along the ground and then place yourself in the line of the ball. Kneel on either knee so the middle of the inside of the foot is in line with the ball's path. The other knee is placed next to the front foot so that there are no gaps for the ball to get through.
2. Then cup your hands in front of the foot. You will move your hands as the ball moves so that the ball enters the hands.
3. As the ball enters the hands the next aim is to try and pick the ball up in one movement and stand up to return the ball.
4. Have the group in pairs with a ball, rolling it along the ground towards each other so they can both practise the long barrier.
5. Progress this so that the ball is being rolled to the side so you have to move yourself into the line of the ball.

Variations

- To challenge the more able in the group encourage them to combine the stopping of the ball and the pick-up into one swift movement and increase the speed of getting down and up.

- Another option, once the basic skill is mastered, is to bounce the ball to each other as this will mean the hands will have to move up or down to allow for the bounce.

Over-arm throw

A step-by-step breakdown of the over-arm throw.

Objective

- To introduce the basic model for an over-arm throw.

Resources

- One ball between two

What to do

1. Organise the class into pairs, with one ball between two.
2. The technique as a whole is somewhat complicated but can be broken down into lots of small, progressive steps.
3. Start by standing 3m away from your partner. To begin with throw the ball to them using *just* your wrist. At this stage it may help to hold the wrist with your other hand.
4. Move back to around 5m. This time, throw the ball using your forearm as well. A good frame of reference here is to think about a darts player.
5. Move back another 3m. This time bring the whole arm in to the arm so that it creates a 90° angle with the body. Try to keep the upper arm relatively still and throw the ball to your partner. Again it may help to hold the arm around the bicep to limit the amount of movement.
6. Finally, move back slightly again so that the distance is around 10m. Start in the same position but move the upper arm back so it starts slightly behind the body. As you throw the ball, bring your arm through, extending it to point towards where the ball has travelled.
7. Allow time to practise the complete movement. In addition to these, for the complete throw the non-throwing arm and or foot can be pointed at the target to help control the body position for a straighter throw.

Under-arm bowling

The basic technique for bowling under-arm as used in rounders.

Objective

- To introduce the basic technique for under-arm bowling.

Resources

- One ball and 5 × 5m of space per pair

What to do

1. If you are right-handed, take the ball in the fingers of your right hand. Take a sideways stance so that the left shoulder is facing towards the batter as this acts as a director (it may be easier to point the fingers of the left hand at your target). Place the left foot straight so that it points in the direction you want the ball to go, and then place your feet shoulder width apart with the right foot positioned to create a 90° angle.
2. Swing the right arm back and slightly bend your right leg. Then swing your right arm through. The angle for releasing the ball will depend how high or low you want the ball to go, but a good starting point will be to say 45° past the hip. Encourage the more able to aim for the ball to stay flat, rather than looping up and down. If you are left-handed then reverse the instructions.
3. The rule for where the ball should be bowled is between the batter's knee and shoulder and within a reachable distance. The best way to practise this is to be in pairs and bowl the ball to each other. After a while, have one partner hold a hoop so it stands just to the side of them between their knee and chin. This will test if the bowler can bowl accurately and will help in the future as it becomes easier to visualise a target.

Variation

- This can be used as a fielding skill for both rounders and cricket, for when you are throwing the ball over a short distance. The throw provides a lot of accuracy (in comparison to the over-arm throw).

Rounders hit

The basic technique for hitting a ball.

Objective

- To introduce the basic technique for striking a ball.

Resources

- One ball, one bat and 5 × 5m of space per pair

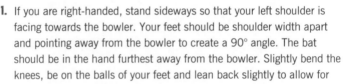

What to do

1. If you are right-handed, stand sideways so that your left shoulder is facing towards the bowler. Your feet should be shoulder width apart and pointing away from the bowler to create a 90° angle. The bat should be in the hand furthest away from the bowler. Slightly bend the knees, be on the balls of your feet and lean back slightly to allow for more movement in the swing.

2. Hold the bat at around waist height above the right foot. As the ball approaches you step with the front foot towards it (the size of the step will depend on where the ball has been bowled) and swing the bat through. As you step your front foot should point roughly in the direction the ball is going. Initially, aim to keep the bat horizontal as you swing through so that you develop greater accuracy. As children develop and attempt to hit the ball for distance, the swing will come from a lower position and contact will be made with the ball as the swing comes higher.

3. Your follow-through should result in your weight being on your front leg and your right arm coming up to the opposite shoulder. It is imperative to watch the ball at all times.

4. Split the group into pairs and have one person throw the ball under-arm for the other to hit. Regularly swap the feeder and emphasise the importance of an accurate feed as you are trying to work on the

batting and not the bowling yet. If you are left-handed, then reverse the instructions.
5. You will have to emphasise to the group that the aim of the hit at this stage is a controlled hit, rather than a strong hit for distance.

Variation

- A good variation is to give the group targets to hit when practising, such as using hoops or marking areas with cones to encourage the group to hit to a clear, specific area in terms of distance and or direction.

Bowling

 The over-arm bowling technique for cricket.

Objective

- To introduce the basic technique for bowling.

Resources

- One ball and 5 × 7m of space per pair

What to do

1. If you are right-handed, hold the ball in the fingers of your right hand. Hold the ball just in front of your chin. A good analogy is to refer to this as being ready to eat an apple. Step forward and place the left foot pointing forwards (as this will help dictate where the ball goes) and the right foot shoulder width behind while also facing forwards.
2. As you bowl, keep your head up and look at where you want the ball to go. Lift your left arm in the air and point this at where you want the ball to go.
3. Rotate the right arm around, keeping the arm straight and fully extended so that it brushes past the ear; as you do, bring the right foot forward, pointing straight, and transfer your weight onto it. The aim is to make the range of movement resemble the shape of the number 6.
4. Release the ball as the arm begins to drop (this will be shortly after the arm has brushed past the ear).
5. The aim is to have the ball bounce before the ball hits the wicket and a good starting point is to aim for the ball to bounce 2m in front of the wicket. The higher the point of release, the further away the ball will bounce, so instruct individually on this basis.

6. If you are left-handed, reverse the instructions.

7. Have the group in pairs bowling back and forth to each other. Start with a small distance of 6–7m then increase the distance.

Variation

- Once the basic technique is correct, increase the distance you are trying to cover, but do this gradually. Then introduce a target, this will ideally be a wicket but something like a chair or hoop will suffice.

The grip

The basic technique for holding a cricket bat.

Objective

- To introduce the basic grip technique.

Resources

- One bat per person

What to do

1. Using the correct grip is essential for all batting strokes and will vary slightly from person to person as they find a grip which is comfortable.
2. The teaching of the grip can be broken down into two steps. Start with the bat face (flat side) down on the ground and instruct the group to place their hands on the handle as if they are about to pick up the bat, but tell them the bat must not leave the ground at this stage (as this puts the hands in 'V' formations, which is needed later on). If you are right-handed, the left hand should be highest and, if left-handed, then the right should be.
3. The next step is to pick up the bat. As you pick up the bat, wrap your fingers and thumbs around the centre of the handle and keep the hands in a 'V' formation. The centre of the 'Vs' should be in the centre of the handle. It is important that the grip is firm but relaxed.

Stance

The basic stance for batsmen in cricket.

Objective

- To introduce the basic stance for batsmen in cricket.

Resources

- One bat and one piece of rope per person

What to do

1. Your feet should be positioned either side of the crease (this is the area just in front of the stumps. If you are not using a crease then you are looking for a distance that gives you enough room to bring your bat back without hitting the stumps). Your feet should point away from the direction of the bowler so that you are side on to them.
2. Both knees should be slightly bent and you should be on the balls of your feet so that you can move easily to where the ball is delivered to.
3. Your bat should start just behind your back foot, but the intricacies of where will vary from person to person depending on whatever feels most comfortable.
4. This is best practised by giving everyone a bat and a piece of rope and using the rope as a crease line. Ask the group to adopt their stance.

Forward defensive

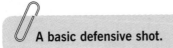 **A basic defensive shot.**

Objective

- To introduce the forward defensive shot.

Resources

- One ball, one bat and 5 × 5m of space per pair

What to do

1. The forward defensive should be used to defend a ball that is on target and uses the basic grip and stance.
2. Watch as the ball is released by the bowler. As the ball approaches and you realise it is straight, move your head and front shoulder in line with the ball, then take a step with the front leg towards the ball so that the foot points towards it. The back leg should remain straight.
3. Bring your bat downwards towards the ball. As you bring the bat down it should be angled downwards slightly so that as the ball hits the bat, it drops to the ground. As the ball hits your bat, your bat should be just in front of your leg, but positioned so that there is no gap between the bat and your legs through which the ball can pass.
4. There is no follow-through with the bat as the aim of the shot is to stop the ball, not to change its direction or add momentum to it.
5. The best way to practise this is to have the group in pairs 5m apart. The ball is thrown under-arm for the batter to practise the shot. As this becomes comfortable, have the ball bounced to the batter. Once this has been mastered, you can have the bowler actually bowling for the batter to practise the shot.

The drive

The fundamentals of the drive shot.

Objective

- To introduce the attacking shot of the front foot drive.

Resources

- One ball, one bat and 5 × 5m of space per pair

What to do

1. Start with the basic grip and stance and watch as the ball is released towards you. Once you have decided where the ball is going to go, move your head and front foot so that they are leaning into the line of the ball. Take a stride so that your front foot points towards where the ball is landing. The front leg should be bent and you should lean forward over this leg so that it takes your body weight as the back leg remains straight. Take your bat backwards slightly (this is your backswing and determines the power of your shot).
2. Then bring the bat down and forwards in a steady continuous action (it is not a swing of the bat). The aim is to connect with the ball as it is in line with your eyes, so that it is just in front of your legs. As you connect with the ball, the gap between your legs and the bat should be as small as possible.
3. As you follow through, the bat should continue so that the face (flat side) of the bat ends up facing the sky.
4. The power of the shot is determined by your backswing, how quickly you bring your bat through onto the ball and how far you follow through. The best way to practise this is to have the group in pairs 5m apart. The ball is thrown under-arm for the batter to practise the shot. As this becomes comfortable, have the ball bounced to the batter. Once this has been mastered you can have the bowler actually bowling for the batter to practise the shot.

Kickball

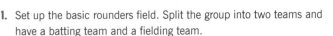

An enjoyable game that works on many of the fundamental skills for striking and fielding.

Objective

- To practise positioning and spatial awareness in a different environment.
- To use fielding skills.

Resources

- A large space, one ball and four bases

What to do

1. Set up the basic rounders field. Split the group into two teams and have a batting team and a fielding team.
2. The fielding team needs a pitcher, a backstop and one person on each base, with the rest of the team spread out as fielders. The pitcher will roll the ball along the floor to the batter who will try to kick the ball. Once they have kicked the ball they must run.
3. The idea works the same as rounders, whereby the aim is to make it round each base. If someone makes it around all the bases in a single go, they score three points, but if they have to stop at a base to make it all the way around, then they only score one point.
4. Have several innings because as the game progresses the understanding and tactics develop. Stress that it is not all about kicking the ball as far as possible and that you want the group to look for gaps in the fielders.

Rounders

An enjoyable game that works on many of the fundamental skills for striking and fielding.

Objectives

- To practise positioning and spatial awareness in a different environment.
- To practise striking and fielding skills.

Resources

- A large space, one bat, one ball and four bases

What to do

1. Set up the basic rounders field. Split the group into two teams and have a batting team and a fielding team.
2. The fielding team needs a pitcher, a backstop and one person on each base, with the rest of the team spread out as fielders. The pitcher will bowl the ball to the batter who will try to hit the ball. Once they have hit the ball they must run.
3. The aim is to make it round each base. If someone makes it around all the bases in single go, they score three points, but if they have to stop at a base to make it all the way around, then they only score one point.
4. Have several innings because as the game progresses the understanding and tactics develop. Stress that it is not all about hitting the ball as far as possible and that you want the group to look for gaps in the fielders.

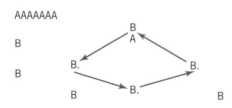

Figure 7.1 Striking and fielding activities – rounders.

Diamond cricket

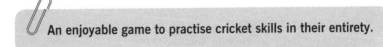

An enjoyable game to practise cricket skills in their entirety.

Objective

- To put the techniques learnt so far into practice.

Resources

- Four bats, one ball, four wickets and a large space

What to do

1. You have four batters standing in a diamond shape with a bowler in the middle. The rest of the children are all fielders. The bowler bowls under-arm at any of the batters – it doesn't matter who or in what order.
2. If the batter hits the ball, they all have to run to the next wicket or they can keep running if the ball is not fielded well. They have to stay in order. They can't overtake. The ball is fielded back to the bowler who bowls straight away even if the batters are still running.
3. A batter is out if caught or bowled and is replaced by one of the fielders. This goes on until all the children have had a bat or time runs out. Each time a batter runs, even if they were not the one being bowled at, they get a run. Each child needs to keep their own score.

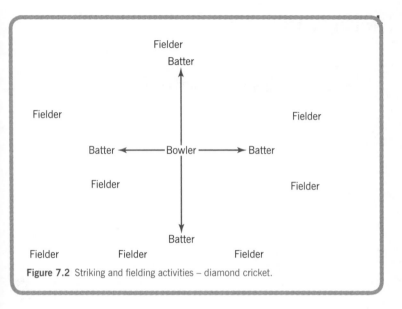

Figure 7.2 Striking and fielding activities – diamond cricket.

Rolling race

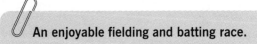

An enjoyable fielding and batting race.

Objectives

- To improve running with a bat.
- To improve picking up a moving ball.
- To improve rolling a ball at a target.

Resources

- One wicket, one ball and one bat

What to do

1. Set up two *creases* (small areas), eight yards apart.
2. Split the class into two teams and designate one as the batting team and one as the fielding team.
3. The fielding team line up to the left of the top crease and the batting team to the right.
4. Roll the ball towards the fielding team. As soon as you roll the ball the first batter has to run (with the bat) to the crease with the wicket. Their aim is to get to the crease before the fielding team manage to throw or roll the ball towards you/the wicket.
5. Ensure everyone has at least one go and then swap the roles of the teams.
6. One point is awarded to whoever completes their task.
7. Encourage batters to slide their bat into the crease.

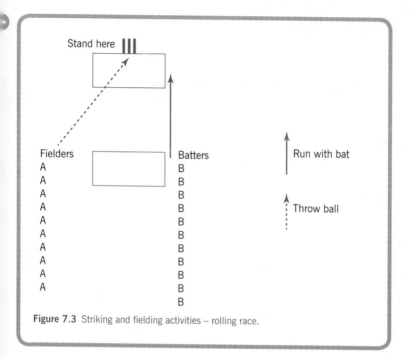

Figure 7.3 Striking and fielding activities – rolling race.

Quick cricket

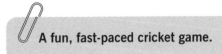

A fun, fast-paced cricket game.

Objective

- To put all of the cricket skills learnt into practice.

Resources

- One wicket, one ball and one bat

What to do

1. Split the group into two teams. Designate one team as the batting team and one as the fielding team.
2. Select one bowler from the fielding team. The bowler bowls under-arm from the bowling cone.
3. Batters try to hit the ball. If they hit the ball they must run around either of the running cones and back. Each time they round the cone and get back, they score one run.
4. Bowlers do not have to wait for the batter to return or to be ready. If the bowler bowls the ball at the wicket, or the batter hits a ball that is caught by the fielding team, they are out and the next batter comes in. A good rule is that batters cannot be out on their first ball.

Variation

- If working with a smaller group do not split into teams. Have everyone field and rotate the batter and bowler as needed.

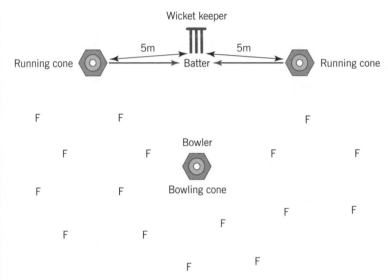

Figure 7.4 Striking and fielding activities – quick cricket.

Chapter 8
Net/wall skills

Racquet control

The fundamentals of holding and controlling a racquet.

Objective

- To introduce the holding of the racquet and basic racquet control.

Resources

- One racquet and ball per person

What to do

1. The actual holding of the racquet is probably the most important element as it can directly affect every stroke you make. The best way to start with the correct grip is to be in pairs. Have one person hold the racquet by the strings and point the handle at their partner. Their partner should then grab the racquet as if to shake hands with it, then keep the racquet in their hand and you have the basic grip for tennis. It is important to hold the racquet towards the bottom of the handle.
2. Once the grip is correct the next step is to use the racquet on the ball. To begin with, start simply. Ask the group to hit the ball in the air as many times as possible with the ball bouncing once in between and then with as few bounces as possible, but ensure you emphasise that you want small hits with the racquet, that big high hits will send the ball out of control and the centre of the racquet gives a straighter and more comfortable bounce.
3. Another similar ball familiarisation skill is to see how many times they can hit the ball downwards (in a basketball dribble motion) and then see if they can do this while moving around.

4. Another challenge is to see how far they can walk or run around while balancing the ball on the strings of the racquet.
5. Once all of these have been practised you can piece them together in relay races. So in teams of four, one person goes first, running while balancing the ball on the racquet to a cone 5m away, does five knock-downs, runs another 5m then does five hit-ups and then runs back to their team and the next person goes

Ready position

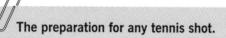

The preparation for any tennis shot.

Objective

- To introduce the ready position for playing shots.

Resources

- One racquet per person

What to do

1. Have both hands on the racquet, with your feet shoulder width apart and positioned so that you are facing the opposition. Have both knees bent and be on the balls of your feet so that you can move quickly and easily.
2. Where possible you should return to this stance after every shot you play and, ideally, come back in to the middle of the court and get in this position so that you can quickly respond to any shot your opponent plays.

Forehand drive

The basic technique for the forehand drive.

Objective

- To introduce the forehand drive.

Resources

- One racquet per person and one ball and a 5 × 8m grid per pair

What to do

1. The forehand shot will be used for shots towards the right-hand side of a right-handed player (and left for left-handed). Holding the racquet in the right hand, take a small step into a sideways stance with the left foot and with the left shoulder pointing forwards and in the direction you want the ball to travel.
2. You should be an arm's length away from where the ball will pass you and towards the left-hand side, as this way you can hit the ball. (This is something that will improve the more an individual plays.)
3. Lift your left arm to shoulder level and have it again pointing in the direction that you want the ball to travel in. Swing the right arm back behind your body as far as possible and then swing the arm through, ensuring that it stays straight. It is important to try and hit the ball with the centre of the racquet as this gives more bounce.
4. Have the group in pairs in a 5 × 8m grid with a person at either end of the grid (to begin with this should be around 4m apart). Bounce the ball with your left hand and then swing and hit with the racquet in your right, as explained above, and aim for the ball to reach your partner. Then progress the pairs to see if they can hit the ball back and forth. Reverse these instructions for left-handed players.
5. I recommend using this practice method as a service, as the overhead serve is too complicated for most at this age.

Backhand drive

The basic technique for the backhand shot in tennis.

Objective

- To introduce the basic technical model for the backhand.

Resources

- One racquet per person and one ball and a 5 × 8m grid per pair

What to do

1. The backhand will be used for shots towards the left-hand side of a right-handed player (or right for left-handed). Watch the ball as it travels towards you and place yourself so you are just short of an arm's length to the right-hand side of where the ball is likely to pass. Take the racquet in the right hand as normal.
2. Take a step across towards the ball with your right foot so that your right shoulder is pointing in the direction you want the ball to go. Bring the left arm back in line with your shoulder. Have the left foot pointing away from the body at a 90° angle.
3. Bring the racquet back towards your left hand and then swing through, ensuring that you connect with the ball in the centre of the racquet.
4. Have the group in pairs in a 5 × 8m grid with a person at either end of the grid (to begin with this should be a around 4m apart). Bounce the ball with one hand and then swing and hit, with the racquet in your other hand, as explained above, and aim for the ball to reach your partner. Then progress the pairs to see if they can hit the ball back and forth.

The volley

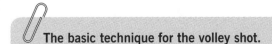

The basic technique for the volley shot.

Objective

- To develop and improve the technique for the complicated volley shot.

Resources

- One racquet each and one ball and a 5 × 5m grid per pair

What to do

1. This shot should be used closer to the net so the ball doesn't bounce and therefore this is slightly more difficult to grasp.
2. Hold the racquet out in front of you at about waist height with your elbow in front of you.
3. Watch the ball and make sure you are within arm's length of the ball. Take small steps to adjust your feet so that the right foot is pointing forwards and in the direction you want the ball to travel. The left foot should be pointing away from the body at a 90° angle. Reverse for left-handed players.
4. Bend both knees and bring the racquet up to where the ball is travelling. The shot doesn't require a full swing, which is why the shot takes place entirely in front of you. The shot itself should be a short, sharp strike with the racquet.
5. The follow-through should result in your weight being on the front leg and both knees should be very bent at this stage and the arm should be stretched out in front of you.
6. This can be practised by standing in pairs about 5m apart with the partner throwing the ball under-arm at about shoulder height for their partner to hit.

Rallies

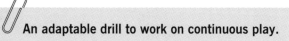

An adaptable drill to work on continuous play.

Objective

- To practise shots in a game-like situation.

Resources

- One racquet each and one ball and a 5 × 8m grid per pair

What to do

1. Have the group in pairs in a 5 × 8m grid, with one person at either end (distances are adaptable to the ability of the group or pair). The pair play a rally between them to see how many hits they can manage before the ball leaves the grid or bounces twice.
2. During the practice you can recap the basic stroke techniques and the ready position.
3. Start with the rule of only using the forehand drive and staying towards the back of the grid and then use only the volley (but bring the pair closer together). Finish by allowing them to use the whole grid and using whatever stroke they like, which then gives them practice in selecting the correct type of shot.
4. Ideally, this should be done over a net, but if this is not available then simply lay a rope on the floor.
5. You can run the drill as a competition for the class to see who can get the most in an allotted time. Alternatively, give the group the task, let them have a go, recap your teaching points and then see if they can beat their previous score.

Are you ready?

A challenging exercise to practise and improve the ready position.

Objective

- To practise preparing for a shot.

Resources

- One racquet and three balls per group of four

What to do

1. Have the group in pairs. Have two cones set up 5m apart and then three cones set up behind one of the cones, as shown in Figure 8.1. The person on the top cone is the feeder and throws the ball to their partner who is on the next cone and is the hitter. The ball is thrown (under-arm) to the hitter, who hits the ball back to their partner. After they have hit the ball they must run back and touch one of the cones and then return to be able to play another shot. Regularly swap the feeder and hitter.
2. Once the group is familiar with the exercise, number the cones and have the feeder shout the number before each shot is played. The hitter then runs to that cone and returns to play the shot. Start with the cones in consecutive order but then change them so that the order requires thought.
3. The teaching point is getting back into the ready positions as quickly and efficiently as possible.

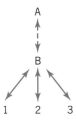

Figure 8.1 Net/wall activities – are you ready?

Turnaround tennis

An enjoyable, challenging drill that works on ready positions and stroke play.

Objective

- To improve ready position and shot play.

Resources

- One racquet and four balls per group of four

What to do

1. Have the class in groups of five. Set up the cones in a compass formation (as shown in Figure 8.2) with 5m between each cone. Have someone stand on each cone with the person in the middle holding a racquet and the others having a ball.
2. The people around the grid are numbered 1–4. Every time you shout a number, the person in the middle turns to the number it is and a ball is thrown to them and they hit it back to the person. Start with volleys as this will be the correct distance and then you can progress it to any shot from a greater distance.
3. Regularly swap the middle person around and you can even swap where each number is to keep the group on their toes.

```
            1


  2         A         4


            3
```

Figure 8.2 Net/wall activities – turnaround tennis.

Rapid rally

A fun drill that works on making shots under pressure.

Objective

- To practise shots under pressure.

Resources

- Two 10 × 5m grids with one racquet per person and one ball per grid

What to do

1. Split the group into four equal teams and have two teams at either end of each grid. The grids should be 10 × 5m with a net (or rope) across the middle.
2. Place a cone 1m behind the back line of each half and have the groups line up. The first person steps forward and hits the ball to the other end for the other team to hit. Once someone hits the ball they run to their left and join the opposite line and the next person in the group comes forward.
3. This is physically taxing as the group is sprinting around, but also works on getting them ready quickly to ensure the quality of their shot.
4. You can do this as a team competition whereby when someone makes a mistake, they are eliminated and so on until all of a team have been eliminated.

| AAAAA | A | | B | BBBBB |

Figure 8.3 Net/wall activities – rapid rally.

Trounders

An enjoyable game for practising tennis shots.

Objective

- To practise shots.

Resources

- A large space, one racquet, four bases and one ball

What to do

1. Set up a rounders field and split the group into two teams. The game works on the same basis as rounders but, rather than using a bat, you use a tennis racquet.
2. Hitters should start in the ready position and hit the ball using one of the tennis shots you have taught.
3. A good idea is to award extra points for technically good shots.
4. If you have a lot of space you can use tennis balls, but if you have limited space (such as being indoors) then you can use sponge balls.

Introduction

The Olympics showcased the best athletes in the world not only in the high-profile events such as the sprints, long jump, long distance running and gymnastics, but also alternative sports such as handball. This section provides some ideas on how to teach some of the skills needed for both volleyball and handball and provides options for adapting the full games to fit the requirements of the primary curriculum and the resources and needs of your school.

Chapter 9
Alternative sports

Volleyball

An adapted version of the full game suitable for upper KS2.

Objectives

- To put volleyball skills into a game situation.
- To practise the serve, pass and dig.

Resources

- Volleyballs (or soft balls) and a net (approximately 2m tall)

What to do

1. Split the class into teams of four (although this can be changed to suit your class).
2. Place a net in the middle of a court which is roughly the size of one-third of a netball court.
3. The essential rules are that if the ball hits the floor in your half then the other team scores a point and if you hit the ball and it lands outside the court then the other team scores a point again.
4. There are lots of variations around rules and conditions to enable children to become more familiar with the game. For example:
   - Start with the rules that the serve must be an under-arm serve (as shown in this book), that at least two passes must be made before the ball can be returned and that a player cannot pass to themselves.
   - Another great condition at the introductory stage is to allow the first and second contact to be a catch and throw. This should be phased out as children become more comfortable with the game.
   - The height of the net and number of touches/passes needed should be tailored to the class or even to specific teams.

Volleyball dig

A simple introduction to hitting a volleyball.

Objective

• To introduce and practise how to hit a volleyball.

Resources

• Volleyballs (or soft balls)

What to do

1. I recommend teaching this after the pass and the serve as you can take parts from both and put them into this.
2. For the dig, place your non-serving (weaker) hand underneath your other hand making sure that both of your palms are facing upwards. As with the serve, the thumb goes next to the fingers, but this time you do not close your fingers to make the fist.
3. As the ball comes towards you swing your arms to hit the ball where the wrist and the palm join.
4. Practise in pairs, with one partner throwing the ball for the partner to hit the ball back into their hands.
5. Next, encourage children to bend their knees and as they hit the ball to push up and extend their legs to generate even more power. Explain that this step will also help in a game if the ball is very close to the floor.

Volleyball pass

A step-by-step approach to teaching the pass (or sett) technique for volleyball.

Objective

- To introduce and practise passing a volleyball.

Resources

- Volleyballs (or soft balls)

What to do

1. Put the group into pairs with one ball per pair.
2. Instruct the group to see if they can pass the ball to each other, keeping it above their heads.
3. Stop the group and model the steps needed for a good pass:
   - Start with your hands on your hips as if you are angry at someone (this always leads to some laughter), making sure you are looking at them.
   - Move the hands to the top of the head as if you create a set of antlers.
   - Move the hand out in front of the head as shown.
   - This is now the ready position for a pass.
4. As the ball travels towards you make sure you are in line with it and move you hands as needed, making sure they are going to make contact with the ball. Stress that this is not a catch.
5. As the ball approaches make sure your knees and elbows are bent slightly and as the ball touches your fingers push gently back against the ball extending both your legs and arms, to pass it to where you want it to go.
6. The force and angle of your hands will dictate the direction in which the ball will travel.
7. Have the class in pairs, practising passing the ball to their partner and then challenge them to see if they can both keep the ball in the air using this technique.

Variation

- If children are comfortable with this you can introduce net or similar obstacles for them to pass over or around.

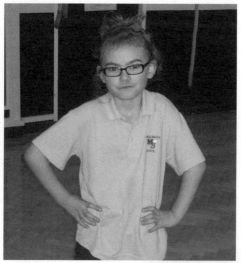

Volleyball serve

A breakdown of how to introduce and improve a basic serve.

Objective

- To introduce how to serve a volleyball.

Resources

- Volleyballs (or soft balls)

What to do

1. Put the class into pairs and have them stand approximately 5m apart with one ball between two.
2. Introduce the under-arm serve. Hold the ball out in front of you just below waist height in your weaker hand. Point the foot (of the same side), in the direction you want the ball to travel. A good tip is to refer to it as the child's writing and non-writing hand/side.
3. Make a closed fist with the striking hand, ensuring that the thumb is against (not underneath) fingers. Swing this arm through, keeping the arm relatively straight and hit the ball using the heel of the hand:
   - If a child is struggling with the part of the hand to use, ask them to close their fist with their thumb against their finger and ask them to find the hardest part. This will be the heel and helps children understand why that part is used.
   - Make sure children continue to swing their arm even after contact with the ball as the followthrough will generate more power in the serve.
4. Have the children in pairs, with one serving the ball for the other to catch and then swapping roles. The timing of when the ball is hit in the swing and the power generated in the swing will dictate the path the ball takes, so children will need to practise hitting the ball at different points and with different amounts of force.

5. Gradually increase the distance between each pair and once the children have mastered the technique, introduce a net and the idea of having to create a looped path for the ball to go over the net and drop down inside the opposition's half.

Handball

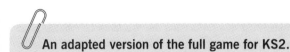

An adapted version of the full game for KS2.

Objectives

- To practise throwing and catching in a competitive situation.
- To demonstrate tactical awareness and teamwork.

Resources

- One soft medium hand-sized ball and cones/goals

What to do

1. The size of the court can be easily adapted to fit the number of children you have but for teams of six, a court the size of a normal hall or $1/3$ of a netball court is ideal. Use cones to mark out a square 4 × 4m in front of the goal as the goal area. Use a soft medium-sized ball.
2. If indoors, I recommend using a small pop-up goal without goalkeepers; if outside I recommend a small football goal with a net, although other goals (including cones) will suffice.
3. The aim of the game is to throw the ball into the opposition's goal.
4. You are only allowed to take three steps with the ball, but bouncing the ball is allowed.
5. Players can shoot from anywhere except the goal area, as only goalkeepers (if being used) are allowed inside there.
6. Defenders are not allowed to hold attackers, strike or pull back an opponent's throwing arm or push an attacker. If they do, the attacking team gets a free throw at the goal from 5m.

Variations

- The actual game makes use of a sin-bin and this is a fantastic tool for games if children constantly intentionally break the rules or for serious offences. It allows the child time to reflect on what they have done, calm down and gives the other team an advantage.
- The game also uses two referees and for upper Key Stage 2 getting the children to referee once they are familiar with the rules is a good way to involve all children and provides a comprehensive sport export experience.

Part 3
Athletics

Introduction

Many of the skills for athletics are very technical, but the underpinning skills and ideas can be developed and practised in smaller parts (chaining). These small parts can be practised individually and then grouped together ready for the whole exercise. A key point to be aware of as a teacher is the safety element. For example, when doing jumping and running exercises, be cautious when judging weather and general safety conditions.

The technical element means that differentiation may be required, which may involve using another adult. Having one adult working on the small parts and the other working on the whole skills may be a beneficial arrangement.

Chapter 10
Athletics

Running

To introduce the fundamentals of running.

Objective

- To introduce the arm and leg movements needed for sprinting.

Resources

- 20 × 20m of space

What to do

1. Split the group into pairs and have them stand 20m apart. Ask them to take it in turns to run a single 20m. Give them two attempts and then ask the group if they know of any way they could increase their speed. Putting the group into pairs will give everyone the chance to actually see the teaching points you make in practice when their partner runs. This also gives the group the opportunity for short rests, which are needed with sprinting.
2. The answer you are looking for is using the arms to help power the legs. Give a demonstration on the spot or running properly as to how much faster you can go when you use your arms.
3. Ask the children to run on the spot with their arms down by their sides, then ask them to run using their arms as well. The difference will be clear.
4. The other possible way to increase speed is to bring the knees higher as you sprint. Again, demonstrate this. Introduce the arm and leg movements separately as this gives everyone the chance to see that both make a difference. Let the group have two attempts with the arm movements before adding the leg movements.

Fast and slow

An enjoyable warm-up for sprinting work.

Objective

- To prepare the group for sprinting work or running-based activities.

Resources

- 20 × 20m of space

What to do

1. Have the group stand inside a 20 × 20m grid. Instruct the group to walk around the grid, travelling in any direction they want to. Then, under your instruction, they will gradually increase the pace at which they are moving. Go from a walk, to a light jog, to a normal jog, to a fast jog and then sprint. The progression to sprint should be staged and you can dip back and forth between speeds.
2. This can be used as a cool-down by reversing the activity, starting with sprints and then gradually decreasing all the way down to walking pace.
3. When doing the sprinting stage, you can recap on the teaching points of sprinting and you can also use these as a method of controlling your speed, because if you know the faster you move your arms the faster your legs go, then you know for a fast jog you don't move your arms as quickly as for a sprint.

Class dash

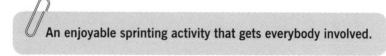

An enjoyable sprinting activity that gets everybody involved.

Objective

- To work on the fundamentals of sprinting and controlling your speed.

Resources

- 20 × 20m of space

What to do

1. Have the whole class together along a line with 2m between each person.
2. Ask the group to stay in position in the line as you move through the activity.
3. Have the group walking forwards, then, on your command, increase their speed. It is best to increase the speed gradually. The distance covered at any one pace should be no more than 15m.
4. You should ensure that during the walk and jogging stages people aren't going faster than they should be, and it is a good idea for the group to stay in a line.
5. This gives people the chance to race against each other and you the chance to work on really powering the arms and legs to create an explosive start at the sprinting.
6. If space is an issue, just slow the pace to a walk or jog and ask the group to turn around and go back the other way.
7. You can also introduce turning into the normal set-up. For example, have the group jogging quickly until you say 'Turn and sprint'.

Speed stations

An exercise involving changing speed and direction.

Objectives

- To introduce running in different directions.
- To improve sprinting technique.

Resources

- 20 × 20m of space

What to do

1. Set up a series of stations 20m apart. Each station requires a different action.
2. Station 1: walk.
3. Station 2: jog.
4. Station 3: run in and out of cones.
5. Station 4: run around a bend.
6. Station 5: sprint.
7. Station 6: fast jog.
8. Station 7: slow jog.
9. Station 8: sprint.

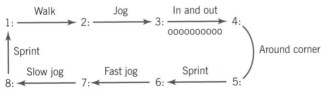

Figure 10.1 Athletics – speed stations.

Variations

- You can change the stations and mix up the order as you feel appropriate.
- Another idea is to add in other activities such as hopping, skipping or jumping.

Cooper's course

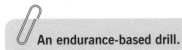

An endurance-based drill.

Objective

- To introduce endurance running.

Resources

- 20 × 20m of space

What to do

1. Set up a 20 × 20m grid with cones at 5m intervals. Each cone symbolises a station. As far as possible, get everyone to start on a different cone. Get the group to run around the grid as many times as possible in five minutes.
2. Everyone must keep track of how many stations they pass, the aim being to pass as many stations as possible in the allocated time.
3. Stress the importance of having a set pace to run at for the whole time rather than just running as fast as you can and then stopping after a minute. The idea of planning a speed, pacing themselves, is actually very difficult and is something that improves with practice.
4. As you are working on endurance, people often find it easier to run with someone else, so don't be too hasty in breaking people up. Only split people up if you genuinely feel it is for the best.
5. You can adjust the time to suit the group.
6. This can be a competition against themselves as they improve on a previously achieved number of stations.

One-footed jump

 To introduce jumping off a single foot.

Objectives

- To introduce jumping off a single foot.
- To determine which foot to take off from.

Resources

- 20 × 20m of space and cones

What to do

1. Mark out a line using cones and have the group stand three steps back from the line.
2. Then instruct the group to take three steps and jump (aim for height rather than distance).
3. For the first two attempts, the first step should be with the right foot (so that you jump off the right leg) and then have two attempts with the first step being with the left (so that you jump off the left leg). Ask the group to compare how comfortable both felt and then ask them to practise the three steps and single leg take-off from whichever leg they feel more comfortable using.
4. As you take your final step before take-off, it is important to plant the foot firmly on the ground so that you can then push against the ground and add more force to your jump.
5. The next part of the take-off will be getting as much power into the take-off as possible. When you take off from one foot, it is important that you really drive the free leg into the air and then bring both arms and the take-off leg up to balance and add more power.
6. Once these are mastered you can then gradually increase the run-up for the take-off. Here you can add the fundamentals of sprinting into the run-up to increase your speed on approach to the jump.
7. This can be applied to the take-off for both high jump and long jump. The key teaching point is to push the body up so that you gain the height you want.

Long jump

The fundamentals of the long jump.

Objective

- To recap the take-off and then add the actual jump.

Resources

- A long jump pit

What to do

1. The take-off foot and take-off technique should have already been covered, so here we are dealing with what to do in the air and how to land safely and effectively. The difficulty with long jump is that each particular stage influences the next, so ensure that each stage is mastered before progressing.
2. You should aim for the jump to be high and long so that you have enough time in the air to adjust your body position to use all of the forward momentum gained from the run-up.
3. As you push your arms up and forwards at take-off, you should lean forward so that your upper body is ahead of your hips. Get the more advanced in the group to reach their arms forward as they jump for extra momentum.
4. Once in the air, extend both your arms and legs so that your body hangs in the air. Tell the group to reach forward with their arms and shoot their feet forwards as they land.
5. The aim is to land so that your feet hit the sand first and then your bottom follows. It is important to remind the group not to put their hands down behind them or walk back through the pit as this would decrease their distance in a competition.

Variation

- If you have to, or want to, do indoor jumps, this exercise can be adapted so that you have a one step or even a standing jump. Here you can teach the take-off and powering the legs and arms into the air and also leaning the body forward. It is important that you get the group to land on both feet for this. Also, use mats for take-off, landing and covering all the floor space in between.

High jump

Introducing the scissor technique for high jump.

Objective

- To introduce the basic scissor technique for high jump.

Resources

- A high jump bar and a high jump bed

What to do

1. The technique for the scissors is often difficult to grasp at first. To begin with, ask the group to find some space, then walk them through the basic technique.
2. Work from just one step to begin with, taking one step then jumping in the air, bringing the free leg as high up as possible (you are aiming for the leg to be horizontal to the ground as you perform the scissor).
3. Then bring the other leg as high into the air as possible. It is called the scissors as the legs imitate scissors in their separation and rejoining.
4. It is vital that on take-off you power the arms into the air as this will generate height and prevents your arms knocking the bar once it is introduced. Once the arms are in the air they will aid balance, so there is no need to bring them down until the landing.
5. Once this stage has been mastered, have them make the step at approximately a 45° angle to the bar. Then put the jump onto the jumping area and allow the group to practise one at a time. Then you can introduce the bar, but start very low and gradually increase the height.
6. Stress to the group that it is the leg furthest from the bar that you jump off, so that if you want to take off from your right foot, your approach would be from the left (as you look straight at it) of the bar and the right for a left-footed take-off.

Variations

- If high jump is being taught indoors, you would focus on the leg drive and support of the arms. Allow for a single-step approach and have the group take off from one foot, jump vertically and reach as high as possible.
- You can have them tag a partner's hand or put paper against a wall and reach as high as possible on the paper. Avoid having pens in hands as this can lead to injury; a good alternative is to use a small dab of paint on the tips of fingers to mark a point. The landing for this should be onto two feet. Again, be sure to use mats.

Overhead throw

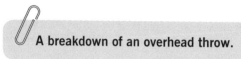

A breakdown of an overhead throw.

Objective

- To introduce the two-handed throw.

What to do

1. This can be used as an athletics throwing activity, for a football throw-in or as a type of pass in either netball or basketball.
2. Hold the ball in two hands so that your fingers form a W shape (see two-handed catch).
3. Bring the ball behind your head so that your hands are at ear level.
4. When you introduce the throw, have children stand with both feet facing forward and with one foot further forward.
5. Bend your knees and back, trunk (torso), neck and shoulders back, transferring your weight onto the back foot. Next, propel your body forward and transfer your weight onto your front foot. Both feet should remain on the floor throughout the throw.
6. Aim to release the ball just as it passes your head. The timing of the release will control the path of the ball.
7. If throwing for any distance, your throw will be powerful, so you should follow-through so that your arms are at full stretch and you are leaning forwards. Your follow-through may result in taking steps forward. It is important to ensure you have released the ball before you step forward and, if throwing in athletics, that you do not step over the throwing line.

Variation

- As children become comfortable with the basic skill, allow them to include a step forward into the throw. As they throw and begin to transfer their weight they can step forward to generate more power for the throw.

Triple jump

A breakdown of how to teach the three-part jump.

Objectives

- To perform a controlled triple jump.
- To combine different jumping and travelling methods. .

What to do

1. This will have to be taught after working on long jump.
2. The first step is decide which foot the child should take off on:
   - Have the children in pairs. The first partner hops as far as they can off their right foot and then off their left. Their partner watches to see which foot produces the longest hop. The partners then swap roles.
   - It is important to explain that a hop is from one foot to the same foot.
   - Explain that they need to flex their knee and drive up and away, using their arms to generate momentum as they do so.
   - It is important that they have decided which foot they feel comfortable and capable of hopping off.
3. The next part is to introduce a step after the hop. Using the same method, the first partner will hop off one foot (landing on the same foot) and take a large step (or stride) onto their other foot. Partners take it in turns.
   - While their partner is hopping and stepping, the other child should be watching them to take or offer advice on how to improve the movement.
4. Recap the skills taught in long jump (see page 196).
5. Have the children take turns at jumping from a standing start as far as they can.
6. Then combine the movements in a hop, step, jump sequence.

My race

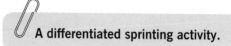

A differentiated sprinting activity.

Objective

- To improve the technique for sprinting.

Resources

- One cone per person

What to do

1. Split the class into pairs and give each child a cone.
2. The first person in each group lines up on the starting line.
3. They then run as far as they can in five seconds. The partner marks out roughly where this is. The children then swap roles and repeat the process.
4. Taking it in turns, children then start at their cone and see if they can get back to starting line within the five-second time limit.

Variations

- The time given can be adjusted with 10 and 15 seconds being good alternatives. As part of the activity partners can use stopwatches to control the time themselves and record the data they collect.
- After 2–3 attempts encourage the children to use their arms to create extra power when they are running.
- For the more able children challenge them to bring their knees higher as they run.

Indoor athletics

 Basic practices for doing athletics indoors.

Objective

- To practise fundamental athletic skills in different ways.

Resources

- Mats, three tape measures, six benches and one ball

What to do

1. This is a series of small indoor athletics ideas. You can combine them in a circuit manner or just progress from one to the next as a class.
   - **Standing long jump**. Use mats and have no run-up, just use a two-footed jump (take off and land on both feet). The teaching points are using the arms to add power and really driving from the knees, pushing down against the floor with the feet.
   - **Standing high jump**. Have a tape measure running up a wall with mats next to the wall. The aim is to jump as high as you can without a run-up. As you jump, tap your fingers on the tape measure. Again it is the powering of the arms and drive from the knees that is important.
   - **Sit and reach**. Have a bench lying on its side on a mat. Sit on the floor with your feet on the flat side of the bench, keep your feet on the bench and have your legs straight, reaching forwards. Then have someone measure how far beyond the knees you can reach. This assesses flexibility.
   - **Harvard stepping**. Place a bench against a wall or wall bars, this stops the bench moving, ensures the children keep their bodies upright and also provides a form of support for the less confident children. The aim is to step up (a foot at a time) onto the bench so that both feet are on the bench and then step down (a foot at a time). Do this as many times as possible in three minutes. This works on endurance, balance and leg power.

- **10m dash**. Sprinting from standing for 10m. This works on the explosive start and powering of knees and arms.
- **Sit down throw**. Place a bench on its side and sit with the soles of your feet against it. Take a football in your arms and throw it with both hands above your head (just like a football throw-in). This works on the angle of release and power of the arms.

Variation

- There are lots of pieces of equipment that can be used for indoor athletics, such as foam javelins. These are generally fantastic and children enjoy using them.

Line running

A fun, team-based running warm-up challenge.

Objectives

- To be physically and mentally ready for a PE lesson.
- To work as a team.
- To develop awareness of running speeds.

Resources

- A netball court (or a similarly marked area)

What to do

1. Split the class into five groups of around six.
2. Position the groups at various points on a netball court.
3. Tell them that they must travel only along the lines of a netball court as a group.
4. Each group starts with ten points, for every 30 seconds they manage not to bump into anyone within their group or another group they score a point. However, every time they bumped into another person they lose a point. The team with the most points is the winner.

Variations

- A good idea is to have each group hold a piece rope to ensure that they stay as a group.
- Another variation is to have a command whereby the person at the front of the group steps to the side and joins the back of the group, so as to ensure that everyone gets a go at making the decision. The sizes and numbers of the group can be altered once the group are familiar with the concept.

20, 20, 20

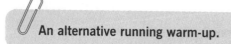

An alternative running warm-up.

Objectives

- To warm up.
- To increase awareness of controlling speed and stride length.

What to do

1. Use an area such as a netball court and have the class moving around the outside it. It may help to spread the class out at the start.
2. Explain what a stride is and tell them that as they are moving they need to count their strides. They need to walk for 20 strides, jog for 20 strides and then sprint for 20 strides. They repeat the cycle for three minutes.
3. Watch to ensure that a clear change of pace and stride length is evident. This also acts as a brilliant starting point if teaching sprinting or running styles.

Part 4
Indoor activities

Introduction

Frequently if PE, and particularly games lessons, cannot take place outside then PE is cancelled or reverts to repetition of one or two activities throughout the year and year groups. Many of the activities in this book can be used indoors or adjusted to fit which is why many of the activities outline a required space of around 20 × 20m. Hockey for example can be easily played and practised indoors by turning benches on their side to create goals to use with Uni-Hoc equipment.

This section includes activities that are indoor activities. There are elements of skill development in the explanations but I would encourage you to start an indoor lesson with a skill introduction (as you would an outdoor) and use these activities to apply those skills in a competitive environment.

Chapter 11
Indoor activities

Benchball

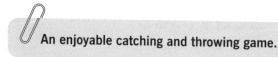

An enjoyable catching and throwing game.

Objective

- To practise the techniques for catching and throwing.

Resources

- 30 × 20m of space, four benches and one bib for every two children

What to do

1. Set up a 30 × 20m grid (but this is adaptable to suit the space you have and the ability of the group). Have two benches (placed together) at the end of each half. Then a line of cones in the middle of the grid to create two halves. Divide the class into two teams and place a team in each half.
2. Select two catchers from each team and have them stand on the benches in the opposition's half. The players then have to throw the ball to their catchers. If the ball is caught by someone on the bench without them falling off, the person who threw the ball joins them on the bench and becomes a catcher as well.
3. Players cannot move with the ball but can pass to team-mates to create a position to throw. When a ball is caught by a catcher it is then just dropped on the floor so the opposing team can continue.
4. The game is won when all the players from one team are on the benches or a set time limit has been reached (15 minutes). In the case of a set time, the team with the most players on the benches is the winner.

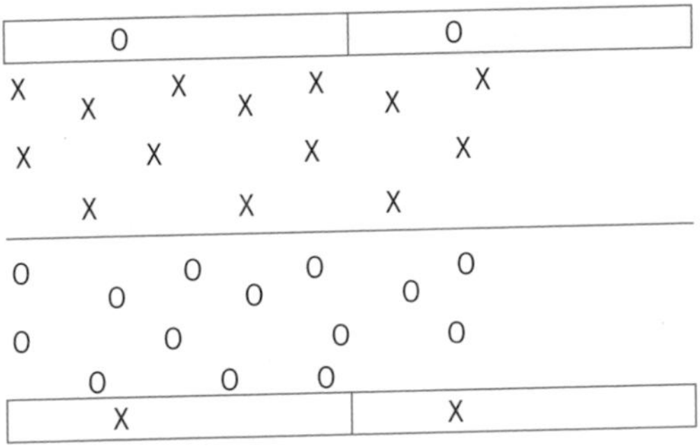

Figure 11.1 Indoor activities – benchball.

Variations

- You can vary the number and size of balls in play depending on the age and skill of the group.
- You can remove the halfway line so that everyone can move everywhere and in doing so practise spatial awareness.
- With both versions you can introduce rules such as five different people have to touch the ball before you can score, having a minimum number of passes or making a rule so that boys have to pass to girls and vice versa.

Dodgeball

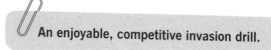

An enjoyable, competitive invasion drill.

Objective

- To practise ball familiarisation and the fundamentals of invasion sports.

Resources

- 20 × 20m of space and four sponge balls

What to do

1. Split the class into three equal teams but only have two of them playing at a time.
2. Have a large area (approximately 20 × 20m) with a line in the middle to create two halves and place a team in each half. Start with four balls (two on either side), but adjust the number to suit the size of the group as you see fit.
3. It is imperative that you use sponge balls, due to the nature of the game.
4. The aim is to hit an opposition player between the waist and toe. If you manage to hit someone between the waist and toe then your team scores a point. If you manage to catch a ball thrown by the opposition before it hits the ground then the opposition lose a point. Any throw you deem to be dangerous (e.g. aimed at someone's head) can be punished with one minute in the sin bin. You as the teacher award the points and sin bins.
5. Play for either a time (ideally five minutes) or for a set number of points (five points) and then rotate the other team into the game.

Variations

- This can be played as an elimination game, whereby, if you are hit, you are eliminated and if you catch a ball, the person who threw it is eliminated and you can save someone on your team.
- Another way is to have everyone inside a 20 × 20m grid with five people spread out on the outside with sponge balls. They then throw the balls at those in the middle. As people are hit, they then go on the side and throw balls at those in the middle. Again, you have to be hit between the waist and toe.

Skittleball

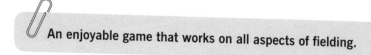

An enjoyable game that works on all aspects of fielding.

Objective

- To practise stopping, catching and throwing techniques under pressure.

Resources

- 25 × 25m of space, ten pins (targets), one sponge ball and one bib for every two children

What to do

1. Split the class into two teams and set up a 25 × 25m grid with a dividing line down the middle to create two halves. Place one team in each half. Then place five targets towards the end of each half. (Ideally you should use pins, but balls on cones will suffice.)
2. While staying in their own half, each team aims to throw the sponge ball at the opposition's targets to knock them over while ensuring that their targets are not hit.
3. Players cannot take more than one step with the ball, but can pass the ball to people on their team.

```
O           A              |        B    B    O
      A                    |
O              A           |    B             O
         A                 |
O              A           |        B         O
      A                    |
O                          |    B             O
         A                 |          B
O                          |             B    O
```

Figure 11.2 Indoor activities – skittleball.

Variations

- You can split each half into two areas so that you have an attacking and a defending area that people cannot move between, but regularly swap the roles people take.
- You can introduce rules, such as everyone must touch the ball, there must be a certain number of passes or you cannot take consecutive throws (to ensure that everyone gets a turn).
- Another fun rule to add in is that if an attacker throws the ball and it is caught by a defender before it bounces, then either the defending team scores a point or the person who throws the ball has a two-minute time out.
- This can be adapted for basketball or netball. Shorten the grid and use the same idea so that people pass the ball at the target but then have to catch it and move while doing so.
- A great progression is to introduce more than 1 ball and this can be done ball by ball to a level the group can handle.

Bench wars

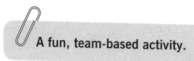
A fun, team-based activity.

Objective

- To improve teamworking.

What to do

1. Set up four benches in a cross formation in the middle of the hall.
2. Split the class and have each team sit on a bench.
3. Instruct them to travel around the hall individually, but that any time you say 'bench', they have to get back to their bench as quickly as possible without jumping or stepping over any of the benches. The first team back is the winner.

Variations

- This activity lends itself to changes. A good adaptation is to have everyone travelling around the hall using different modes of travelling.
- Another alternative is to have half of each team travelling clockwise and the other anti-clockwise.
- Rather than just sitting on the bench on return, you can have standing, balancing on one leg or any similar variation.
- To further develop teamworking you can challenge them to arrange themselves in order according to height or age order.

The channel crossing

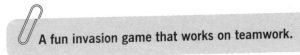

A fun invasion game that works on teamwork.

Objectives

- To develop tactical thinking.
- To improve teamworking.

What to do

1. Set up a river in the middle of the hall by marking out a 2m-wide channel with cones or rope.
2. Select one or two volunteers to start as the catchers in the river and place them in the channel.
3. The rest of the players start at one end of the hall and attempt to make it to the other side without being tagged. If they are tagged by a catcher, they join the catcher.
4. Repeat the process until only two people are left.

Variation

- Sort the class into small groups, so that if anyone from a team is tagged, the whole group becomes catchers as well. A good idea is to start with one pair and when they tag someone, they swap roles.

Scooch it

An enjoyable, indoor team game.

Objectives

- To work as a team.
- To practise throwing and catching.

What to do

1. Place benches turned on their side at opposite ends of the hall. Lay a mat in front of each bench.
2. Arrange the class into teams of approximately seven. If you have a larger class you can either rotate players in or rotate teams.
3. The aim is to throw the ball so that it hits the flat face of the bench.
4. The rules are that everyone (except the goalkeeper) must remain with their bottoms on the floor. Goalkeepers must remain on their mat. You cannot move with the ball. Tackling is not allowed but interceptions are. Any breaking of the rules is punishable by a free throw, which means that the opposition get to restart with the ball on the halfway mark.
5. Tell the class that they do not have to shoot all of the time, as they can pass to their teammates.

Variations

- You can introduce additional rules such as: at least three passes must be made or you can only shoot when past halfway.

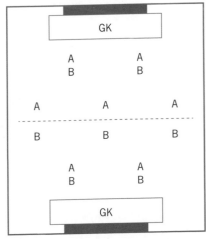

Figure 11.3 Indoor activities – scooch It.

Minefield

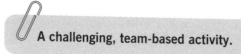

A challenging, team-based activity.

Objectives

- To improve teamworking.
- To improve communication skills.

What to do

1. Split the class into groups of six.
2. Make an area and subdivide it into smaller sections in a 5 × 5 set up to create the template. On paper replicate this grid and draw a path from start to finish.
3. The first person in the group steps towards the grid while the rest of the group sit facing away. If a child steps on a square they shouldn't, say 'stop'.
4. If a child doesn't make it through, they speak to the next person only.
5. When a child is attempting the field, the rest of the group must be silent.

Variation

- Use small whiteboards and let children create routes for each other. You can also use different sized grids to suit your class.

START

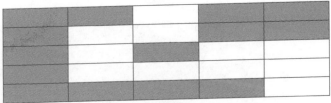

FINISH

Figure 11.4 Indoor activities – minefield.

Part 5
Outdoor and adventurous

Introduction

Outdoor and adventurous is an area of PE that if often overlooked, but when taught well, will be viewed by children in as high regard as the traditional areas of PE. Outdoor and adventurous is designed to practise and improve leadership, communication, teamwork and logical thinking through solving real physical challenges. The module will also develop map-reading skills and gives children who are not as sport-oriented as others a chance to excel and shine in PE through the area's cognitive requirements.

Chapter 12
Outdoor and adventurous

Raging rapids

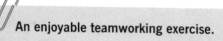

An enjoyable teamworking exercise.

Objective

- To get groups to work as a team to solve problems.

Resources

- Two mats and two benches per group (plus additional benches for progression)

What to do

1. Have benches set up at either end of the hall and split the class into groups of four with two mats and two benches per group.
2. Have the groups stand on the mats and explain that everyone in each group must get from one bench to the other as quickly as possible without touching the floor (as this is water). Instead, they must use their mats to get across the hall (water).
3. There are many approaches to doing this and the aim is for the groups to devise a method and execute it themselves.

Variation

- To progress the exercise, you can introduce obstacles such as benches laid across the floor that the group then has to travel over using their mats.

Bench games

Enjoyable activities that work on organisation and teamwork.

Objective

- To practise teamwork and organisational skills.

Resources

- Three benches

What to do

1. Split the class into three groups and have each group stand on a bench. (If your school has houses, then it is ideal to use these to divide the group and then award points for achievements.)
2. Tell the group that everyone has to stay on the bench, but they have to organise themselves into height order, tallest to shortest. If anyone falls off the bench, then a three-second penalty is incurred. The first team to do this wins. Then ask them to reverse the order, i.e. shortest to tallest.
3. You can use height, age or alphabetical order of first or last names.
4. After a couple of attempts, tell them they cannot speak during the exercise, thereby making them find new ways of communicating.

Word hunt

An enjoyable teamworking game that works on communication

Objective

- To develop teamworking.

Resources

- Five word hunt cards

What to do

1. Split the group into five teams and name each group after a colour. Have the groups sitting in a straight line in a corner of the room.
2. The exercise requires you to create cards (as shown right). Each card is numbered. On each card there is a table with the column headings of group, letter and next station. The cards should be scattered around the room and can even be hidden.
3. Each group is given a starting number. The first person leaves the group and goes to the number they have been given. They then return to the group, tell them the letter(s) and tell the next person which number they have to go to. This continues until the group has all the letters. They then have to put the letters together (as they are not given to them in order) to discover what their word is. The first team to know their word wins.
4. Each team will end up with a different word and the words can be based on a topic they are studying. (You can even make them work out which topic.)

Variation

- You can say that as a person rejoins the group they can only talk to the next person.

CARD 1

Group	Letter (s)	Next station
Red	v	3
Green	us	2
Blue	e	5
Orange	ec	4
Pink	N	6

The subject for this example is Year 6 Science with the topic of forces. The words the letters relate to for each group are gravity, upthrust, resistance, direction, Newton.

Alpha hunt

An enjoyable orienteering activity that works on logic, teamwork and communication.

Objective

- To improve teamworking and logical thinking.

Resources

- One map of the school per pair

What to do

1. Put the group into pairs and give each pair a map of your school grounds. On the back of the map, have the letters of the alphabet listed down the page with space by the side of each letter for them to write next to it.
2. The pairs then have to go off and look around for things that begin with each letter of the alphabet, but must stay together at all times. When they find an object, they mark the letter on the map and then write what the object is on the back of the sheet.
3. You may have to manufacture some examples, such as putting a ¼ sign in a window so that they can use quarter for Q (you can be as creative as you like with these). The first group to have an answer for all 26, or whichever has the most answers when time is up, is the winner.
4. You will see some groups going through the alphabet, so they look for something for a, then b, then c and so on, while others will look around and then write down what they see. Do not encourage or discourage either or any other way as the idea is that the groups come up with their own ideas and this can be used as part of an evaluation or plenary.

Orienteering

A teamworking activity that works on orienteering skills.

Objective

- To work on teamworking, map-reading and logic.

Resources

- One map of the school per pair and a pack of playing cards

What to do

1. Divide the group into pairs and give them a map of the school. On the map you will have marked a series of 'X's, at which you will have placed a card (from a normal pack of cards). Each map has a different X circled as the starting point.
2. The pairs move around in whatever order they like, but ensure that groups do not simply follow each other. If they do follow each other, simply circle another X for each group to go and find.
3. Once they have made it to all the stations, they then come to you and check that the cards they have written down are correct. The first team to find all of the cards, win.
4. The cards can be hidden at the X (such as in a bush or on a tree).

Variations

- You can work in groups of up to five and to make sure they stay as a group, give them a rope that everyone must hold at all times.
- You can arrange it so that each time a card is discovered, the group comes back to you (or another adult) and they are given another X to go and find. This system helps you to keep track of how each team is doing and avoid teams simply following each other.

Untangle the knot

A fun activity that requires logical thinking and team working.

Objectives

- To work as a team.
- To develop logical thinking.

What to do

1. Split the class into groups of approximately six.
2. Everybody puts their left hand into the circle and holds someone's hand. Then everyone puts their right hand into the circle and holds a different person's hand.
3. The challenge is to untangle the knot without releasing any of the handshakes.

Variation

- If this is achieved within the small group, increase the number of children in the group. It is possible to do this with an entire class.

Pass the hoop

A fun, simple teamworking challenge.

Objective

- To work as a team member.

What to do

1. Get the group to stand in a large circle.
2. Place a hula-hoop on the arm of a child and then instruct everybody to hold hands with the people either side of them.
3. Challenge the group to pass the hula-hoop around the circle without breaking the chain.

Variation

- A fun variation is to have more than one group and play it as a competition with a time penalty any time the chain is broken.

Leapfrog

A logical thinking activity for upper Key Stage 2.

Objectives

- To develop logical thinking.
- To work as a team.

Resources

- Seven hoops per group
- Two sets of different coloured bibs

What to do

1. Divide your class into groups of approximately four and lay out sets of cones and hoops as shown.
2. Instruct the group that they have to move the cones so that the red cones are where the yellow cones are and vice versa.
3. Introduce the rules that cones can move forward or backwards one space into an empty hoop or jump over a cone if the next hoop is empty.
4. Challenge groups to do this in as few moves as possible.

Variations

- You can vary the number of cones and hoops.
- A very good progression is that when a group thinks they know a method and can recall it, replace cones with children and see if they can complete the challenge. Changing the object often changes the recall and thought process.

Figure 12.1 Outdoor and adventurous – leapfrog.